Confessions
of an Imperfect
Mom

Julie Barnhill

HARVEST HOUSE PUBLISHERS

EUGENE, OREGON

Cover illustration © iStockphoto/girlfrommars

Cover by Dugan Design Group, Bloomington, Minnesota

Published in association with the literary agency of Alive Communications, Inc., 7680 Goddard Street, Ste #200, Colorado Springs, CO 80920. www.alivecommunications.com.

CONFESSIONS OF AN IMPERFECT MOM
Copyright © 2006 by Julie Ann Barnhill
Published 2011 by Harvest House Publishers
Eugene, Oregon 97402
www.harvesthousepublishers.com

Library of Congress Cataloging-in-Publication Data

Barnhill, Julie Ann, 1965-
   [Motherhood]
   Confessions of an imperfect mom / Julie Ann Barnhill.
      p. cm.
   Originally published: Motherhood. c2006
   Includes bibliographical references.
   ISBN 978-0-7369-2951-6 (pbk.)
   ISBN 978-0-7369-4157-0 (eBook)
   1. Mothers—Religious life. 2. Guilt—Religious aspects—Christianity. 3. Motherhood—Religious aspects—Christianity. I. Title.
   BV4529.18.B37 2011
   248.8'431—dc22

                                                                    2011008906

Printed in the United States of America

11 12 13 14 15 16 17 18 19 / VP-MS / 10 9 8 7 6 5 4 3 2 1

Contents

To
Patrick,
Ricky Neal,
and Kristen.
I delight in your company and
wouldn't change a thing.

Acknowledgments

Many thanks to the leadership and countless volunteers who make up the fabulous organization known as Hearts at Home. Its fearless leader, Jill Savage, gave me an opportunity to present a workshop at their national conference in 1998, and we've been working as a team ever since.

As always (and forever), love and gratitude to my husband, Rick Barnhill, and our three incredible spawnlings: Kristen, Ricky Neal, and Patrick.

And of course, Anne Christian Buchanan—an editor par excellence! Working with you has been a professional treat, and you consistently sharpen me as an author and woman.

Last, but *never* least, Harvest House Publishers. Thank you, Bob Hawkins Jr., for believing once again in a message—my message in particular!—of humor and heart. What a delight to work with Terry Glaspey, LaRae Weikert, Carolyn McCready, and Betty Fletcher. And where, oh where, would my author self be without the savvy leadership of John Constance, Barb Sherrill, and their sales and marketing teams? Finally, a monstrous thank you and acknowledgment to the people at Harvest House who consistently deliver book orders on time and with a spirit of joy.

What We've Done Right

Stop Now and Read This First!

◎

After a particular speaking session in 2004, I knew what the opening salvo of this book needed to be.

The occasion was a MOPS (Mothers of Preschoolers) meeting. I had just spoken on the topic of motherhood and anger with just a few words about guilt added in, and the women broke off into pint-sized discussion groups. Watching them cluster together, I glanced down and considered the discussion questions I had suggested:

1. Do you ever find yourself looking to an author, teacher, or speaker for an ever-elusive final answer to your mothering problems?

2. Have you ever believed (or do you believe today) that *good* moms simply do not have (or discuss) certain feelings and situations?

3. Does regret and guilt take up a large or small portion of your thinking as a mom?

Gazing up from my sheet of paper, I began overhearing snippets of conversation from the groups:

"I rarely feel absolutely sure about what I'm doing as a mom."

"You mean it's possible to be a mom and *not* feel guilt?"

"My daughter is three years old, and I seriously think I've ruined her for life."

Ack! At this point I shouted for attention and changed the discussion rules altogether.

"Okay, ladies, we're going to have a slight change of plans here. Instead of discussing the three questions on the paper I gave you, I want you to turn the sheet over and answer one question only: 'What do you *not* feel guilty about as a mother?'"

Well, you'd have thought I'd asked for nominations for the ugliest baby contest!

Absolute silence ruled in that small basement room.

No one spoke.

No one wrote down a thought.

No one moved.

You've got to be kidding me, I thought. *These women can't think of anything they've done right as mothers? How sad is that?*

I gently prodded, asking the women to recall special times spent with their children or to think back to the day before or even that morning and share at least one guilt-free moment of joy, laughter, confidence, and grace. And still we waited...until at last one brave soul volunteered, "Well, I don't feel guilty for giving my two-year-old son lots of hugs and kisses. Is that what you mean by something not being on my guilt list?"

Yes! That was exactly what I meant. And with that one guilt-free admission, the dam burst wide open. One after another, the moms spoke up.

"I don't feel guilty for not cooking dinner every night."

"I don't feel guilty for saying 'I love you' a million times a day."

"I don't feel guilty for not wavering on discipline."

"I don't feel guilty for not giving up."

"I don't feel guilty for limiting the number of children I have."

"I don't feel guilty for nursing my babies past nine months."

"I don't feel guilty for saying no."

"I don't feel guilty for putting my children's daddy first."

Each confession seemed to embolden the group as one toddler-draped mom after another approached me afterward and expressed her thanks for being *forced* to recall the things she had done right.

And that, in this book about imperfect motherhood, is where I want to take you first. Before we even survey the mountainous landscape of Guiltmore National Park, which I believe looms on the horizon of every mother's life, I want you to take a good, solid look at what you've done as a mother that inspires absolutely no guilt at all.

I see you now, sitting with book in hand, hoping with everything you're worth that this will be it—the one book that will reassure you, answer all your questions, explain your screwups, and solve your worries and regrets. Perhaps you are ready to relay a hundred, a thousand, maybe ten thousand specific examples of what you have done imperfectly and why you feel so lousy about them.

If that's true, then this book's for you.

But not this chapter. See, this chapter is all about you and me facing the seemingly inexplicable reality that we *haven't* done everything wrong. That we all take many actions that are not only harmless but actually wonderful and wise. In fact, we have innumerable memories squirreled away in the quagmire of our maternal minds that are full of light and life, that indicate a mothering life well considered.

This is where I want us to begin.

Before we grapple with the various peaks of guilt and regret that loom on the landscape of our lives, I want us—I want you—to create that list of everything you have done right.

And I do mean everything. I'm not playing around here, girls.

This is serious business—motherhood—and more than anything else I want us to start our time with one another on the right foot. I don't think you need another author telling you what, in her opinion, you've done wrong as a parent. And you certainly don't need me to add to your already (I'm sure) lengthy "I've Got Guilt" list.

No, as is the case with 99.9 percent of what I write, speak, and believe, my primary objective is to assure you right here, right now, that you are not alone.

You're not alone with your crippling guilt.

You're not alone when you second-guess nine out of ten things you decide.

And you're absolutely not alone when you do a great job as a mom—despite your many reservations.

Don't be surprised if making your list is a bit more difficult than you first expected. After all, when we assess our parenting skills, most of us have learned to think negatively rather than positively. Most of us could easily list 20 things we feel guilty about for each thing we did right. So take your time and think things through. But don't try to analyze or dissect…just think of and list the things you have absolutely no guilt for doing, saying, or believing. They can be simple little specific things or big parenting policies. Small triumphs or big satisfactions. Things you don't think were wrong and things you're convinced were absolutely right!

Just in case you've wondered, here are just a few things that aren't on my personal guilt list.

- Having children so early into my marriage.

- Asking a million questions regarding the health of my children (gestational development, weird rashes, apnea fears) and getting second and third opinions.

- Picking my babies up every time they cried.

- Going away on weeklong vacations without kids.
- Letting my kids watch *SpongeBob SquarePants*.
- Saying, "Because I said so!" a dozen times a day.
- Admitting I hate to play board games.
- Belting out classic rock-and-roll tunes at the top of my lungs while stuck in traffic with three irritated and irrational children. Go Huey! Long live Journey!
- Saying "I'm sorry" time and time again.
- Baking chocolate-chip cookies nearly every week for the past 17 years.
- Admitting when I'm wrong. (It does happen on occasion.)
- Living as authentic a life as possible.

Making a list like that feels wonderful! It manages to silence, if only briefly, the clanging refrains of shoulda, coulda, and woulda that ring in the air around most mothers I know. Me in particular. But you too.

So now it's your turn. Grab your pen and start writing. Remind yourself of the many things you have done right. If you have to, start with the basics like "I don't feel guilty for providing my children with food and shelter and clothing." Then move forward from there. And if you find yourself coming up short…well, pick up the phone and call your mother, sister, spouse, girlfriend, or even your own child, and let them tell you what to write.

What isn't on my guilt list as a mom: _____

_____

(Come on—you can list more than that!) _____

_____

_____

_____

_____

(Try to think of two or three more. You can do it.) _____

_____

_____

_____

_____ *(Perfect!)*

Now, take a minute to read back over what you've written. Pretty nice, huh? Nice and eye-opening, actually.

What I've Done Right

I don't feel guilty for singing to my daughter, making sure she has soft, downy pillows and covers on her Bed, and allowing her to splash to her heart's delight while taking a Bath.

—Anita, age 25

Truth is, we have all done innumerable things right. But all too often those details get relegated to the back corners of our memories. It's all too easy to forget the sweet, sane moments when engaged in day-to-day, year-after-year battles with fussy newborns, peevish toddlers, anxious preschoolers, squirrelly 11-year-olds, and hormonally raging teenagers—perhaps at times when you're feeling fussy, peevish, anxious, squirrelly, or a bit hormonal yourself! That's why I've included more—*lots more*—"What I've done right" examples scattered throughout the book. I gathered these from hundreds of surveys completed by real moms just like you and me. Just reading them has helped me as I grapple with the reality of motherhood—guilt, regret, and second-guessing. I hope they'll help you remember even more of what you've done right. I also hope you'll keep your own list close at hand as you proceed through this book. Read it often to remind yourself of who you are as a mom—and who you can be.

I'm trying to do that too because I don't believe there is another mother who could be any harder on herself than I am. Making a conscious effort to remind myself of what I've done right hasn't always been on the top of my to-do list.

It is now. And I hope you will do the same because we have nearly 200 pages of material to cover with one another, and a few of the mountain peaks of guilt we have to contend with are going to be exhausting. It would be easy, perhaps, to become discouraged and simply give up. Or to think we've ruined our kids for life and beat ourselves up over the things we should have done, could have done, or would have done if we'd only known better.

Sigh.

But you don't have to do either of those things—give up or beat yourself up—because you can experience life beyond guilt. You can settle into motherhood with your confidence restored, your regret dismantled, and your doubt and second-guessing diminished to an occasional whisper.

I know because these days I even manage to experience that from time to time.

My oldest child, Kristen, is nearly 23 years old, and many of the stories you will read are about me figuring out how to parent a strong-willed female who resembles her mother oh, so much. Her 21-year-old brother, Ricky Neal, who now towers over me by more than a foot, finds plenty of time in the spotlight as well. You may remember Ricky Neal from my first book, *She's Gonna Blow!*[1] And then there is my youngest, 16-year-old Patrick Michael, who has questioned why my previous writings did not include more tales about him. Ah...this book's for you, buddy! Indeed, Patrick has helped me accrue more than a fair share of "third child" regret and guilt. I hope he's benefited even more from my more recent excursions into guilt-free territory.

No, that wasn't a typo you just read. There truly is an ultimate destination of guilt-free, joyful mothering! And we're going to get there together. You see, ladies, I speak from hard-fought experience. I know the landscape of mothering guilt like the back of my hand. I've also begun to explore the far more beautiful vistas of Graceland—and I'm not talking about Elvis here!

No, Graceland is a place of refuge, relief, and hope for all mothers, and I'm privileged to lead you there and share with you a few observations and lessons I've learned along the way.

1
The Mountain Range in Your Backyard

Acknowledging Guiltmore

◎

My children have an impatient, quirky, hardworking, verbose, affectionate, opinionated, forgiving, occasionally cranky, and ever-so-slightly neurotic mom who loves them madly. A neurotic mother who over the gamut of her mothering experience (twenty-two years, five months, twenty-eight days, seven hours, seventeen minutes, and sixteen seconds) has often belabored the minutiae of mothering life.[2] Trust me—no trivial detail has escaped the proclivities of my maternal angst.

It officially started in January 1988 as I pored over pregnancy and medical reference books, hoping to discern if the formation of my first child had in any manner been compromised due to my consuming celebratory glasses (yes, *plural*) of Asti Spumante approximately six hours prior to her, um…rather unexpected conception. (We shall always consider Kristen to be our honeymoon souvenir gift.)

A few weeks afterward (it seems), I was slathering coconut butter on my ever-expanding belly and courageously attempting to swallow prenatal vitamins roughly the size of a man's big toe each morning before eating breakfast and leaving for work.

I was absolutely determined to do everything right with my pregnancy and as a mother.

That's why I began the first of many conversations with my baby when she approximated the size and shape of a small lima bean. An article in *Perfect Mother* magazine had convinced me that any hope of a successful nurturing of the mother-child bond depended on the baby's ability to hear and recognize my voice. Hence my daily conversational ramblings.

I talked and talked and talked. Actually, I haven't stopped talking since.

And she was an excellent listener—back then.

Yes, I was determined to do everything right. I cut back—way back—on my daily consumption of Pepsi, refused to walk (or breathe) within a hundred-yard radius of a cat litter box, and carefully measured the width between slats before settling on a beautiful, *safe* cherrywood crib. In addition, having read *The Womanly Art of Breastfeeding*, I began "preparing" those womanly mammary glands for active duty. (It involved sandpaper and sure-grip pliers—we'll leave it at that.)

I read other books as well. Magazines too—a lot of them. Over the course of nine months I purchased, borrowed, and inhaled reams of written material. What information I couldn't find there, I asked of other mothers.

Was it normal for hair to grow exponentially on one's belly while pregnant?

Could the baby sense when I was worried, fearful, or enjoying sex? (The possibility of the latter *really* freaked me out.)

Should I have a water birth, sit on a birthing stool, or strap my legs into stirrups?

Was it bad to want as many pain-numbing drugs as possible—during the seventh month of pregnancy?

Would the fact that I never qualified for National Honor Society hold my child back intellectually?

In light of said academic reality, should I purchase the *Baby Einstein* encyclopedia set with annotated appendixes for the low cost of $15,397.22—a mere $6.89 less than my entire teaching salary for the year, but sure to guarantee that lima-bean baby would qualify for the ranks of MENSA?

Were ankles roughly the size of Babar the elephant's a positive or negative indicator regarding pregnancy weight gain?

What I've Done Right

I kept my family together and taught my children the value of honoring a commitment.

—Janice, age 41

And how would I ever be able to determine when I was in real labor? (Okay, I was slightly neurotic and altogether clueless!)

I had the minutiae of anticipatory maternal neurosis down to a science. By the second trimester I had considered (obsessed over) the following:

Would I be able to interpret my baby's cries?

Would I bump her head into the doorknob while carrying her in my arms?

Would my milk come in?

And more troublesome still—upon careful examination and comparison of two-dimensional breast-feeding diagrams with actual breasts (mine)—how on earth were my now monstrous-sized mammary attachments going to fit within the minuscule circumference of a newborn baby's mouth?

These were the things that kept me up at night! As well as the even more basic worries that haunted me throughout those early months.

What if my baby didn't like me?

What if I didn't like her?

What if I did it all wrong?

A View of Guiltmore

And that, of course, was just the beginning. It was my first glimpse of the mountainous terrain that looms over every mother's life. My first view of the familiar and foreboding range of peaks I've come to call Guiltmore National Park.

You won't be able to locate Guiltmore on a Rand McNally travel atlas. Nor will a list of websites appear after you enter certain keywords in Google. But it's there—this mountainous range of regret, second-guessing, and doubt that can only be seen, observed, trekked, and experienced from a mother's backyard.

It's a familiar sight where most of us live. And it still looms for me, even though my lima-bean baby is now in adulthood with her brothers close behind her. And many days I still find myself trekking the rocky slopes of Guiltmore, pondering questions that range from the mundane to the momentous:

- Was this cavity the result of too many juice boxes when he was little?

- Should we have let her quit piano?

- Was I wrong not to have purchased him drums sooner?

- Did going to public school (instead of the very expensive Christian school or continued homeschooling) hurt our children's chances for college?

- Did all our moves make our children flighty and insecure?
- Do my children have temper tantrums now because I had anger problems when they were growing up?
- Because I let them sleep late on summer mornings (so I could get some writing done), did they struggle with laziness?

Ever found yourself there?
Questioning everything you do as a mother?
Doubting every choice you've made?
Second-guessing past actions?
Agonizing over possible future mistakes?
Beating yourself up over the kind of parent you've turned out to be?

Well, just as one can't have Oreos without a glass of cold milk or even dare to imagine Mary Kate without Ashley, some things just go together. And all too often—let's say *most* often, shall we?—motherhood is accompanied by the nagging, sometimes debilitating emotion of guilt, with that tired trio of regret, doubt, and second-guessing thrown in for good measure.

It Comes with the Territory

Guilt seems bundled within our XX chromosome mothering genes. And some of that guilt is good. Really. Like physical pain, it serves a purpose: It alerts us that we have done something wrong.

But as you've no doubt discovered, mothering guilt can also be a big problem. A looming, mountain-sized problem that clenches our stomachs, robs us of sleep, erodes our peace, and poisons our relationships. How can we ever live as God intended when we're always huddled in the looming shadows of Guiltmore?

Read over the first paragraphs of this chapter, for goodness' sake. It is guilt that keeps panicked mothers up at night, guilt that hinders our decision making and undermines our confidence, guilt that has us feeling defeated before we ever dilate past four centimeters.

And guilt is a widespread phenomenon. In fact, if you enter the keywords *motherhood* and *guilt* into Google, you'll find about 125,000 direct leads to books, magazine articles, websites, blogs, and message boards that all address the topic. I've found through my own less-than-Gallup-style polling that the subject of guilt and mothering is second in interest (and angst) only to anger and motherhood.

This doesn't surprise me in the least. As the high priestess of all reformed angry mothers—my particular Guiltmore has volcanic origins—I know all too well the caustic cycle of uncontrolled anger, regrettable fallout, and guilt. Not to mention guilt that comes from simple carelessness. And guilt that comes from factors beyond my control. And guilt that I manufacture in my own worried mind. It's because the slopes of Guiltmore are so familiar to me that I am attempting to add one more voice to an already busy conversation.

What I've Done Right

Going to my son's room prior to sleep and having a conversation about his day. It is our special time to talk.

—Cheryl, age 44

So here you have it—my own Guiltmore travelogue. It's my account of how I managed to move beyond guilt toward grace and why I think you can get there too. Acknowledging the presence of guilt is simply the first (and key) step in climbing our way past the many regrets, doubts, and shoulda-coulda-woulda realities of being a mother.

But note that I used the phrase "climbing past" rather than "forever conquering" or "utter annihilation of" guilt.

You see, for more than two decades—ever since those lima-bean days—I have awoken to equal parts mothering mayhem and mothering bliss. And there hasn't been a day go by in which something wasn't said, or done, or thought, or forgotten, or screamed, or denied, or remembered, and held hostage by guilt.

Not one day.

I suppose the vast majority of guilty issues were miniscule, seemingly insignificant matters—it pains my head even to attempt to name them. But they were there—those irritating, unsettling, restless feelings of messing up, of not doing and getting everything right. And there are the larger-than-life guilt packages made up of the shamefully painful mistakes and errors in my mothering that I will not even speak aloud.

I have come to believe that I will never be completely rid of guilt as a mother, and I think that's true for you too. I consider guilt, with all its intrinsic ties to maternal life and love, to be a vast, take-your-breath-away, geographical landscape that will sit squarely in my backyard until the day I die. (Comforting thought, eh?) That's why I make no promises of "conquer your guilt" or "break free forever and ever" within the pages of this book. I am *so* over thinking I can do the impossible—and then feeling even more guilty when I cannot.

Yes, guilt will always be part of the mothering landscape.

But pay attention because this is important: It doesn't have to *dominate* your landscape. It doesn't have to ruin your life, or spoil your fun, or rob you of peace of mind. More important, it doesn't have to erode your confidence and cripple your effectiveness as a mother and a human being.

Instead of hunkering down under Guiltmore's shadow, you can learn to scale her slopes and move on to where you were really meant to live—on the sunny plains of grace and confidence. And from there—take it from me—the view is really terrific.

But you can't get there by yourself. (Oh, I suppose you could try, but it's far safer and enjoyable to travel with someone else.) Guiltmore's peaks are too slippery and too treacherous to be navigated alone. They are fraught with danger, and only a trained guide who has traversed their crags of guilt and terrain of mistakes (real and imagined) can lead you safely to those promised vistas of grace and confidence.

You need, in fact, the expert guidance of a sherpa, someone to prepare the way toward the place where you can enjoy loving your children more and dealing with guilt less and less.

I am that sherpa, ladies!

Yes, me. And don't think I don't know what an unlikely candidate I am for the job. I'm the sherpa who took a writing retreat a few years ago to the mountainous peaks of the Colorado Rockies. Let's just say I went, I saw, and was totally uninspired. (Not that there's anything wrong with the Rockies, mind you; I'm just the type to draw my inspiration while sunning on the shores of a white-sand beach, that's all.)

Nevertheless, I'm volunteering for the job.

I will trek ahead and scout for danger and scenic views.

I'll keep an eye out for the hidden crevasses that can swallow a guilt-ridden mother whole.

I'll keep careful watch over threatening mothering conditions that can pile up and trigger an avalanche of despair.

And I'll stay with you until the very end. Of that you can be sure.

All that's left is for you to firmly tighten the knotted rope of motherhood that joins us, grab a pick or two to help you break up some encrustations of false guilt, and prepare to loosen anything and everything that holds you back on the pathway toward grace. Together we're going to scale Guiltmore's peaks and rid ourselves of useless guilt that keeps us from more confident and joyful—yes, joyful!—mothering.

2

A Base-Camp Confession

Lots of Stuff I've Felt Guilty About, For, or Over

All right, raise your hand if you totally skipped "What We've Done Right" and turned to this chapter instead.

Come on…I know you're out there.

It's time for confession and a little turning from your wicked reading ways. So let's have every head down, every eye closed—no one looking around—as you raise those guilty hands, ladies. Okay, I see that hand. Yes, thank you…I see that one as well. How about you in the balcony?…Yes, yes, thank you for your honesty. Is there anyone else, anyone else who would say, "Yes, Julie, I disregarded your introduction and skipped here first"? Ah, one more. Thank you, ladies. There are hands waving all around…

Now, how did I know you were out there?

Pretty simple, really. You did exactly what I would have done.

I'd consider two factors if purchasing a book about motherhood and guilt. First I'd wonder whether the author is an actual living, breathing mother of children. That may seem obvious, but you and I both know there are people out there in the world of books and public speaking who are doling out all sorts of advice and wisdom on subjects they are not qualified to speak on.

I once attended a workshop titled "How to Have a Debt-Free Marriage." The room was packed with financial losers like me, and we were eager to hear *the* answer to our problems. The speaker was introduced, and as she made her way to the lectern I heard audible gasps all around me. I gasped too, when I realized a 13-year-old girl was making her way to the microphone. Well, okay, she may have been 18. But she sure looked a lot like the babysitter I'd just paid $195 to watch my three kids while I attended the seminar.

Seriously, this workshop leader was *very* young. And before she could even make her opening statement, one of my fellow conferees raised her hand. "Excuse me, Miss," she asked kindly, "but how old are you, and how long have you been married?"

Uh…she was 20 years old and had just celebrated 11 *months* of blissful matrimony.

Gulp.

Needless to say, that child's—er, woman's—authority to speak on debt-free marriage was slightly diminished.

Just the other day a friend of mine called and asked if I was the one leading a writer's workshop in California telling authors how they could get on *Oprah* with their books. Now, I did appear once on the *Oprah* show, but I definitely don't lead seminars about it. So I told my friend all this, and she shared with me what she had heard about the workshops.

Well, that stirred my curiosity. Not a bad idea, I thought. I'll go check out this other writer's website and see when she was on the show. Maybe we could compare notes.

So I Googled and surfed my way to her website.

And guess what?

You guessed it. She's never appeared on *Oprah* as a guest. Needless to say, her authority to speak on this subject was vastly diminished in my eyes.

My Qualifications: A Brief Summary

So, back to imperfect motherhood guilt—the first thing I'd want to know before reading a book about it is whether the author has children. And whether they are currently on speaking terms with her. Now, if you had actually started with "Read This First," you'd already know the answer. But for the sake of clarification I shall repeat my kids' names, ages, and current speaking status.

When I wrote this book, my daughter Kristen Jean Barnhill was 17—closing in on 18. And yes, she actually spoke with me, as in "Can I have twenty dollars for gas?" "Would you mind buying me a new pair of jeans?" and "Will you and Dad be paying for my college tuition?" (Little twinge of guilt right there.)

My son Ricky Neal Barnhill was 16 and good to go with such open communication as "Are you and Dad going to buy me a truck?" "Why can't I have a later curfew?" and this little heart-attack inducer: "You can use the money you were saving for college. I've decided to be a drummer in a band instead."

Gasp—someone pass the oxygen, please!

And my son Patrick Michael Barnhill was 11, and, since the moment of his birth, has never stopped talking in some form or fashion with me or with anyone else.

So that should settle concern number one.

The second thing I would want to know if I were purchasing a book about motherhood and guilt is whether the author has actually experienced guilt as a mother and, if so, what exactly she felt guilty about.

Details, author! Give me all the gory, shallow details!

I see you smiling and nodding. You too have watched one too many episodes of *Survivor* and *Nanny 911* and refuse to settle for anything less than honest details. Because really, haven't you ever read a book or listened to a speaker who alluded to some big, dark stain of sin or shame in her life but would never, ever just come right out and say exactly what the sin was? So all the time you're sitting there thinking, "I wonder what she did that was so bad." Doesn't that just annoy the heck out of you? It does me. I say either tell me what it is or don't bring it to my attention in the first place—because I'm never going to be able to follow you to the wrap-up portion of your message where you tell me how that big, dark stain of sin or shame no longer has a grip on your life.

If you don't give me the details, I'll be left thinking you're a mass murderer or that you pilfered DIRECTV for the past ten years!

So that's exactly what I'm going to give you for the rest of this chapter—the specific guilty details that have tied me up in knots over the past 23 years of mothering. I think you'll agree after reading through them that I am more than adequately equipped to speak on the subject of motherhood guilt.

Sherpa Mom's (Partial) Guilt List

- Laughing hysterically when one of my potty-training children slipped bottom first into the toilet—legs pointed skyward, arms flailing. More guilt: I still laugh out loud picturing it.

- Putting Kristen in her Johnny Jump Up, where she dislodged a hanging plaque while bouncing and was hit just below her right eye.

- Never managing to have a cool tree house built for my kids.

- Leaving Kristen for the first time in a church nursery on October 16, 1989. (I document all my neuroses, remember?)

- Giving my children really bad at-home haircuts.

- Leaving a bottle of cold medicine with codeine out on a countertop. Kristen drank an unknown quantity, and I had to call poison control.

What I've Done Right

Staying home with my kids even though that meant working odd jobs like housecleaning and babysitting. We were poor, but my children tell me they never knew it. I fixed cheese and pickle sandwiches! They thought they were gourmet meals.

—Karla, age 52

- Not nursing Ricky Neal—I quit as soon as it hurt.

- Spending less one-on-one time with baby number two.

- Being irritated (after I knew the kids were okay) when I had spent money for an unnecessary doctor's visit.

- Enrolling Ricky Neal in preschool even though I knew he was too young because I was intent on getting a few hours all to myself.

- Leaving Ricky Neal with family members (so I could take my husband to the hospital for surgery) and not being home to spot a bad ear infection that perforated his eardrum.

- Taking Ricky to a hearing screening due to developmentally delayed speech. I just knew the delay was due either to that ear infection or the fact that I hadn't read to him enough.

- Not setting up savings accounts early on with each child.

- Selling all my baby stuff instead of packing it up one more time for a cross-country move.

- Having one (yes, just one) professional photograph taken of Patrick between his birth and his fifth birthday.

- Harshly accusing Kristen as she held her baby brother: "What did you do to make him cry?" The next week I learned that

Patrick's startled cries and gasps were related to severe sleep apnea—not a mean sister.

- Not setting up college funds for our three children.
- Never having a beloved family pet that waited for the family on the front porch steps.
- Being able to travel to cities and countries my children (and husband) have never had the chance to visit.
- Dreading bath time (the kids', not mine!).
- Allowing Ricky to ride his bicycle without shoes. (He nearly severed his pinkie toe as a result.)
- Not buying the kids light-up tennis shoes. (At the time, I didn't think we could afford them.)
- Following a doctor's instructions unquestioningly although his advice clashed with my maternal instincts. (Turned out he was wrong.)
- Spending hundreds of dollars for Creative Memories scrapbooking material, but actually completing six pages over the course of eight years.
- Yelling at my children in public.
- Making a huge deal out of potty training with my firstborn. (Never again!)
- Clipping Patrick's toenails too short when he was a baby and making him bleed and cry.
- Putting off shoe shopping for my kids to the last possible moment. I found out later that one of them was wearing shoes two sizes too small.
- Realizing all three of my children can quote large portions of the *Austin Powers* movies.

- Laughing at my children's *Austin Powers* quotes.
- Kristen's friend telling her she's learned to check the expiration date on all refrigerated items when eating at our house.
- Taking the cash my young children got in their birthday cards. (Kristen got wise around age nine; she started putting hers in a Ziploc bag and hiding it from me.)
- Choosing a homeschool reading curriculum that was too regimented and not geared toward Ricky Neal's style of learning.
- Not serving my family more fruit and vegetables.
- Not being able to help my kids with math problems past addition, subtraction, multiplication, and division.
- Losing my creativity in the kitchen. ("Hey, kids! Who wants cereal for supper...again?")
- Buying whole-grain bread twice in the first 19 years of marriage and motherhood. (Yes, there is a theme here. Remember this for chapter 8.)
- Drinking too much Pepsi and not enough milk when I was pregnant.
- Never reading the complete *Chronicles of Narnia* aloud to my two older children.
- Two words: head lice.
- Discovering a nonpesticide solution (The Licemeister—buy one online today!) years *after* slathering my two oldest children with the toxin a family doctor prescribed. (Remember that guilty confession about not following my maternal instinct?)
- Throwing away ugly Christmas tree ornaments my children made.

- Experiencing female jealousy when I look at my daughter's youth—more specifically, when I look at her taut, firm thighs!

- Leading the Schwan's man on. (I just don't have the heart to tell him I'm not interested in the home-delivery ice cream and overpriced frozen-food items he's trying to sell me.)

- Missing Patrick's tenth birthday because I was speaking on a cruise ship headed to the Grand Cayman Islands. My daughter, Kristen, went with me, but no Patrick. Let's talk *major* guilt, shall we?

- Feeling guilty for *not* feeling guilty when my husband, Rick, and I went on a weeklong vacation and left toddlers Kristen and Ricky Neal with a wonderful friend and caretaker, Sherry Cunningham.

- Hiding certain food items from the kids so I didn't have to share.

- Having a low tolerance for noise. Maybe it has something to do with growing up as an only child. But I'd take the kids over to Gayla English's house and realize my house sounded like a mortuary compared to her lively household. And she almost always seemed calm in the midst of it. Hence my feelings of guilt over silencing my children too often.

- Screaming at my kids (especially during the first five years) when I got frazzled.

- Sometimes wishing I'd never had children.

- Forgetting that Ricky Neal's prescription medicine made him highly susceptible to sunlight and allowing him to go fishing with Kristen and her friend. (He came home with a horrific sunburn, which worsened over the next two days.)

- Not being much of a family photojournalist. We have random photographs, but future generations will be hard pressed to gather much information about the Barnhills based on what few pictures I've taken or purchased.

- Taking the family to Disney World on Christmas Day, 2003, because I had been told by a very reliable source, "It's one of the lowest attended days of the year!" Um, no it's not. The kids rode three rides over a seven-hour period, and Patrick nearly passed out from the fumes emanating from Mickey Mouse's pits as he stood by him for a photograph. Hm...not quite the vacation I had planned.

- Not being able to afford one of those huge wooden play structures that were so popular in the late '90s. My two boys would have loved one.

- Taping over a video of Kristen and Ricky making their first snowman.

- Giving up homeschooling and putting the kids back in public school—second semester—because I needed to go back to work to make ends meet financially. I interviewed for jobs to no avail and ended up substitute teaching—occasionally. All that stressful change for me and the children for less than a thousand dollars. Guilt, guilt, guilt!

- Checking out mentally from my family when working on a book deadline. This one included.

- Finally admitting during the summer of 1999 that I'd rather someone slowly push a dull pencil through my left eyeball than have to sit through one more game of T-ball. (It's one of the main reasons I chose not to have any more children.)

So there you have it, girls—Julie Ann Barnhill in some (not all) of her mother-guilt glory.

From the mundane to the serious, I've accrued more than my fair share of shoulda-woulda-couldas. So on this point I believe you'll agree I am amply qualified to assume Sherpa Mom status. When it comes to guilt, I know the terrain.

A Final Qualification

Which brings me to the third thing I'd want to know when purchasing a book about mothering and guilt, which is whether the author has *learned* anything in her personal trek through Guiltmore. I mean, obviously you want a sherpa who has been there, but you probably don't want a sherpa who's still lost up in the hills!

So I do want you to know that, though Guiltmore still looms in my backyard too, I absolutely don't live there. In fact, when I look back, "What I've Done Right" appears just as large as my shoulda-woulda-couldas.

Through age, experience, some hard work, and some *massive* applications of forgiveness and grace, I've managed to reach the point where I can blow off (many of) the little things, trust God for the big things, and enjoy both my life and my family. As I mentioned—at the moment at least—all three of my children actually speak to me. So does my husband. I consider this a tremendous accomplishment! And the fact that we laugh a lot together is simply gravy.

Another way of saying this is that I know from experience that Graceland really exists. I know it because I've been there. In fact, I live there most of the time.

And no matter what your personal guilt is like, I know you can live there too.

And trust me—you'll love it.

3

A Base-Camp Lecture

The Geography of Guilt

Okay, you're ready to get on the trail. So am I…almost. Just bear with me a little longer while I give my little talk about the geology of the Guiltmore range.

And yes, I hear those groans. You didn't come here for a lecture. You just want to get past your guilt.

Believe me, I understand.

But there are a few things about the makeup of these mountains that you should be aware of before we begin our journey together. I wish another mother would have communicated these geological basics to me years ago when I was all but overwhelmed by those bulleted guilt statements you read in the last chapter. If they had, my first trek through Guiltmore would have been a lot more sure-footed.

So let's take a minute to examine what these mountains are made of. In other words, what exactly does the word *guilt* or the phrase *feeling guilty* mean?

You won't get far along the trail before you discover several different kinds of guilt and some guilt that isn't even really guilt at all.

Now, don't roll your eyes when I say that. Let me explain.

One of the first things I like to do when attempting to understand a word or concept is to refer to the tried-and-true resource of *Webster's Comprehensive Dictionary.* So let's start there.

I'm thumbing through my trusty home dictionary, and this is what I read next to *guilt:*

1. The state of one who, by violation of law, has made himself liable to or deserving punishment; culpability.

2. Wrongdoing; wickedness. See synonyms under *sin.*

Whoa. There's some strong wording for you: *wrongdoing, wickedness. Sin?* So I decide to look up the same word on my computer at Merriam-Webster OnLine, and here's what I read:

1. the fact of having committed a breach of conduct especially violating law and involving a penalty; *broadly* : guilty conduct

2. **a** : the state of one who has committed an offense especially consciously **b** : feelings of culpability especially for imagined offenses or from a sense of inadequacy : SELF-REPROACH

3. : a feeling of culpability for offenses.

As you can see, there is plenty of room for discussion regarding the type of guilt you and I are dealing with as mothers. Some guilt is a *fact*—actual wrongdoing or even sin. Some guilt is a *feeling*— which might not involve actual wrongdoing at all. Outcroppings of all these kinds of guilt form the rocky landscape of Guiltmore, and the park trails are also strewn with elements of fear, anxiety, shame, and regret. Most important, different kinds of guilt and guilt feelings call for different mountain climbing techniques. So we're going to need to know a little about the different kinds of guilt if we ever hope to reach those vistas of Graceland.

The Power of Thinking Differently

During the first six years of my older children's lives, I was a volatile mix of frustrated, anxious, impatient, and furious mothering. I loved my children passionately, yet they also seemed to have an uncanny knack for pushing my buttons and setting me off. And they had a hard time knowing from day to day exactly what would set me off. To be honest, so did I. There were more days than I care to admit when an ambiguous "something" was all it took to send me exploding in anger, as well as plenty of days when Kristen or Ricky Neal would act in some completely normal manner and precipitate an angry outburst.

At the time, I didn't understand the vast difference between childish behavior and willful disobedience. Or the equally vast difference in how a mother should respond to each one.

Simple, huh? Perhaps you knew this early on as a mother or picked it up within a relatively short period of time. I sure wish that had been true for me; it would have made a big difference. Because for months and years I treated and reacted to nearly all childish behavior as willful disobedience. I rarely, if ever, really thought through and considered what my expectations should be for Kristen and Ricky in relation to their ages. I rarely, if ever, cut them any real slack. Instead, I demanded unrealistic behavior and abilities from my children who were, when all was said and done, mere children.

What I've Done Right

Teaching my kids about Jesus.

—Natalie, age 25

Once I realized that certain things would occur and could be gently and lovingly dealt with according to my children's age and ability, life became a whole lot sweeter and a lot more fun.

What does all this have to do with guilt? Simply that a change in our basic understanding can make all the difference in changing our feelings and our behavior. And the basic understanding that has helped me most in trekking through Guiltmore is that 99.9 percent of the items and details of my guilt list meet the *second* definition for the term *guilt:* "feelings of culpability especially for imagined offenses or from a sense of inadequacy."

Yes, that would be me!

Time and time again, I have been a mother held hostage by feelings of culpability for imagined offenses and by a sense of my own inadequacy. There are very few examples in the aforementioned list or in the pages you are about to read that qualify under the first *Webster's* definition of wrongdoing, wickedness, or—*gulp*—sin.

Not that I'm *incapable* of wrongdoing and sin! Far from it. But the truth is that my guilt over real sin and wrongdoing is hopelessly mixed up with my guilt for imagined offenses.

I *felt* guilty and inadequate for not having a cool tree house for my kids to enjoy. But it wasn't really wrong, wicked, or a sin not to have one.

I *felt* extremely guilty and inadequate for leaving a potentially poisonous cough medicine open and within my daughter's reach. I did not, however, do it out of some wicked choice to harm my daughter.

I *felt* guilty and inadequate for serving my family so few fruits and leafy green vegetables. But it really wasn't wrong, wicked, or a sin to do so. (Note: Please don't write me angry e-mails of dissent if you do feel this was wrong, wicked, or a sin. Instead, offer a simple prayer to God that oranges and broccoli will somehow come to look as appetizing to me as a bag of M&Ms and a plateful of russet potatoes.)

True or False

Are you beginning to get my point here? Let me phrase it in another manner.

You have probably read or heard other men and women speak on the subject of guilt. And most, if not all of them, had a clever catch phrase to help you distinguish the kind of guilt you're dealing with. You may remember a few of them:

Good guilt and bad guilt.

Productive guilt and nonproductive guilt.

Chronic guilt and episodic guilt.

Social guilt and religious guilt.

Blah, blah, blah, blah, blah. (I almost feel guilty for not listing the remaining 10,387 examples I have!)

For me, though, the most helpful descriptions speak of *true (or real)* and *false* guilt. True guilt involves actually doing something wrong or failing to do something right. False guilt is a matter of imagined offenses.

The trouble is, it's often hard to tell the difference—just as it's tricky to take a quick look at a mountain peak and know what kind of rock it's made of. (Well, maybe that's not hard for you, but it is for me!) That's because both kinds of guilt can feel the same—which is just awful!

And that brings us to a helpful point, which is that *feeling* guilty is not necessarily the same thing as *being* guilty. How can you distinguish between the two? Author, speaker, and radio host Mary Whelchel gives this helpful advice:

> True guilt is specific. You know why you're feeling guilty and what you're supposed to do about it. False guilt is a vague, cloudy feeling, one that's tough to nail down. It says, "I'm not right. I'm not what I should be."[3]

Now that's a description I can get my mind around! It's also where we begin as you encounter the multitude of guilts that clutter Guiltmore's many trails. At some point you'll need to examine each and every one and ask yourself, is this guilt true or false? Do I know why I'm feeling guilty for this particular thing, and do I know what I'm supposed to do about it?

What I've Done Right
Teaching my children that character counts!
—Sharon, age 50

If the answer is yes, then you are dealing with true guilt. You can actively pursue the "supposed to do about it" part and move away from its power to weigh you down as a mother.

However, if upon closer examination of a specific guilt you are unable to nail down why you're feeling guilty and you don't really know what you can or should do about it, then in all likelihood, you are dealing with false guilt—which needs to be treated in an entirely different way. (We'll be exploring that in a later chapter.)

Let me use a couple of items from my past as an example.

I have felt guilty for harshly disciplining my second son when he was younger. I would go to bed with a stomachache and wake up with a nagging sense of shame. Now, had I applied Mary's test for determining real or false guilt, I would have asked myself the following:

Do I know why I feel guilty for this particular thing?

The answer would be yes. I knew exactly why I felt guilty. I knew I had gone too far physically in my attempts to discipline Ricky Neal, and I knew I needed to stop any and all physical aggression against him. I knew it was wrong. I knew I felt wicked. And yes, I knew it was a sin.

Hence, true guilt. True guilt that could be remedied and relieved by confessing my sin to God, asking Ricky Neal for forgiveness, and stopping the acts of aggression toward him. (All of which I did.) We'll look at this process later in more detail.

I have also felt guilty for not purchasing a set of drums earlier than 2004 for Ricky Neal. Let's apply Mary's test on this guilt as well:

Do I know why I feel guilty about this situation, and do I know what I am supposed to do about it?

Huh…no, I don't know why I feel guilty about this, not really. I've wondered if maybe I've stunted his talent by taking so long to buy the drums. (He's really good!) And I've wondered if I should have said no to some things I purchased for Rick or myself in order to have been able to purchase them sooner. But then again, I don't really… How's that for vague and cloudy? How's that for feeling "I'm not right because I didn't"?

Hence, false guilt—and something I need to chuck over the first summit I come to!

At this point, though, you may be peering quizzically at the sample guilt-rocks that I've passed around the circle and thinking…I still can't tell the difference.

That's all right.

Truth is, even with Mary's helpful rule of thumb and my own insightful explanation, distinguishing between true guilt and false guilt—or between specific guilt and vague guilt, or whatever—can still be tricky. We can't always trust our feelings or our perceptions or even some of our beliefs, although we shouldn't ignore them either. So it's not always clear what we should do about the guilt that shadows our thoughts and keeps us up at night.

But that's all right too. Some things are more easily learned through hands-on experience. Which is why Sherpa Mom is prepared to end the lecture and get on with the adventure.

When we've had a closer look at the peaks of Guiltmore, we'll have a far better idea of how to put them behind us.

PART TWO

Exploring the Terrain

4

The Foothills of Wasgonnabe

The Trouble with Expectations

◎

Around the time my oldest child hit her thirteenth birthday and the youngest hit his seventh, I realized I really wasn't a "kid" person. Now, why it took me nearly 36 years of life to figure this out, I don't know. The signs were there long before I ever lactated.

Consider, for example, my rather dismal track record with baby-sitting.

It was the fall of 1980, and I was in serious like with one Michael Patrick McHugh. (Is that not a stand-up name to die for? I doodled it on every spiral notebook I possessed and ended up giving my third child—no relation, mind you—a similarly strong name.) A recent transplant to our school from the sunny state of Florida, Mike was a tall, shy, and handsome twelfth grader who actually seemed to like me—a short, loud, and spunky ninth grader.

Life was great that year except for the fact that I was not allowed to car date until I was 16. I was left therefore with no dating alternative other than cruising hand in hand with my beloved during classroom breaks at school.

Sigh.

The situation was not exactly conducive to romance (my parents' thought exactly!). But I was ever the optimist and seized every available moment to enjoy Mike's company...to be in his presence...to simply exist in his same atmosphere.

Which leads me back to that fall evening in 1980.

Earlier that day, I'd accepted an offer to babysit at the home of Evil Spawn I and II. I think their names were Danny and Beth. Or something like that. But "Evil Spawn" reflects their true nature.

I don't know what possessed me to say yes to the proposition. I had deferred time and time before—as had the entire babysitting population of Brunswick, Missouri. But for whatever reason, I found myself attempting to corral said spawn and counting down the hours until their parents returned.

If they returned.

Midway into the evening, the phone rang.

It was my mother telling me that Michael Patrick McHugh had just called *(He's never ever called before!)* and asked if he could come over to my house *(Be still, my hyperventilating heart!)* and see me *(He likes me—he really likes me!)*, but *(Oh! no! Please tell me you didn't!)* she had let him know I was supervising the set of *The Little Shop of Horrors* and was of course unable to see him because of my responsibilities.

Oh, the horror, indeed!

What were the chances that the one time I acted upon pseudo-maternal instinct by accepting a babysitting job, I would torch my love life in the process? What were the chances that after the one six-hour period I spent with children, I'd want nothing more to do with them?

But it wasn't as though I had never enjoyed being around kids.

After all, I had volunteered to work at the local Head Start program with my best friend, Cindy. I had taken care of the infant daughter of the local supermarket owner. I would, upon occasion, play house with the ragtag team of girls on Buchanan Street and volunteer myself as The Mother. If I remember correctly, though, I never held on to that position for long—Lana Lybarger always managed to successfully lead a coup with her rally cries for a more peaceful, compassionate, Monopoly-lovin' brand of mothering.

What I've Done Right

I always found room for one more stray dog, cat, wounded bird, or traumatized rabbit that my children brought home. My kids know what it means to show love and care to animals. We have prayed for their healing, and I'll never regret the time or energy it took to take care of them. All four of my children have wonderful, big hearts, and I like to think this had something to do with it.

—Nancy, age 48

As I said, in hindsight, perhaps some things should have stood out regarding me and children. But I was never actually anti-child. I just thought I'd get better at it (being patient, wanting to play board games) when I had my own. In fact, by the time I married and was actually ready to reproduce, I had some pretty high expectations for myself as a mother and for what kind of family life I would be able to create.

What Happens to Expectations

The trouble is, I thought mothering would be a whole lot easier physically, emotionally, intellectually, and spiritually than it turned out to be.

Up until I actually gave birth to my firstborn, in fact, everything *was* pretty easy.

I got pregnant on my honeymoon night despite contraceptive measures—easy.

With a lone exception involving a sausage, egg, and cheese Hardee's biscuit and a long drive to work, I suffered with little hormonal sickness—easy.

I sailed through those nine months with nary a hint of a problem.

Finding the perfect baby crib—easy.

Shaving my legs up until delivery—easy.

Handing in my teaching resignation so I could stay home—easy.

Lamaze classes—easy.

Inducing labor early to honor my husband's job transfer date—easy.

Labor—eas...

Um, this is where the terrain of mothering expectations began to take a decidedly difficult twist. (It twisted much earlier for some moms dealing with infertility or difficult adoptions.)

Labor most assuredly was not easy. And I was royally ticked during the entire process.

Breathing through my nose was not easy and did not stop the pain.

Being checked for dilation by no less than two former college classmates was not easy. (And yes, they were licensed nurses.)

Attempting to turn from my back to my side was not easy. Nor graceful. Nor, I imagine, easy to watch.

And pushing, minute after minute, time after time, through one contraction after another, was without a doubt the most strenuous activity in which I had ever engaged—definitely not easy. And when our Kristen finally arrived, all seven pounds, three ounces of her, I said aloud, "Well, raising her has got to be a lot easier than giving birth to her."

Can you say *clueless*?

It's been said a journey of a thousand miles begins with a single step. Well, I've come to believe a mothering guilt trip of a thousand miles begins with a single expectation, and you'd better bet some of us are staring slack-jawed at the imposing peaks of Guiltmore, stunned at the reality between what we expected (and expect) for ourselves as mothers and what our mothering life is really like.

Consider these words of a fellow mountaineering mom:

> I always wanted to be a mom. While others were dreaming of being a nurse, a schoolteacher, or an astronaut, I dreamed of being a mom. I had done tons of babysitting as a teenager and young adult. I was single until age 29, and even after getting married I was still asked to babysit for friends. I was so sure that I'd be an awesome mom and quite natural at it—a perfect mother, even. But I couldn't have been further from the truth! I've wondered more than once why God even saw fit to make me a mom.

Sweet women such as this come to the stirrups and adoption table with more than one impossible-to-meet expectation for their lives as a mom. We all do. It's nigh impossible to get through life without forming some concept of who we think we'll be as mothers. And honestly, I think I would fear the woman who somehow managed to do so. I'd think she just didn't care.

Imagining how you'll be as a mom and hoping you'll be a good one is normal and natural. Women have done it for generations, although the specifics of what that means has changed. I was part of a female generation that grew up listening to commercials telling me because I was a woman I could bring home bacon and fry it up as well. In those days, ERA wasn't simply a liquid detergent! And I have photographic proof of my first foray into "I am woman; hear me roar" fashion. There I am in my "power suit" (a polyester blend pinstriped fabric with shoulder pads the size of Mt. Rushmore, a high-collared blouse with a floppy tie at the neck, and businesslike [ergo ugly and definitely nonsexy] pumps), ready to hold forth in a man's world.

At that point in my life, mothering wasn't really on my mind. But when I got around to it, I just knew I'd do it right!

What "Doing It Right" Means

I think we can safely say that many of us grew up in an era when motherhood as a calling wasn't held in high cultural esteem. Yet even during that particular window of history (say 1972–1980), millions of girls somehow managed to dream about the kind of moms we'd like to be.

We would gently but firmly shape our young children's minds. We would feed them nutritious and delicious meals (can you say, "Gourmet baby food"?) and heroically protect their innocence and their self-esteem. We would lead by example. We would study all the experts and avoid all the mistakes our mothers had made.

At least—I wince to remember—that's what I thought.

Admitting this is painful, but a lot of what I always imagined I would be as a mom was based on my determination to not be or not do things the way my mom did.

Shocking, huh?

And I never thought I had the worst mother on the face of the planet. No, I could have easily offered a name or two for that honor. That wasn't the case at all. I just seemed to believe (those many years ago) that she simply wasn't doing things right.

In my mind, *right* pretty much entailed her doing things my way. I persisted in this thinking up until—well, you know, until I had children of my own.

Just last night my husband, Rick, and I were sitting out in our garage watching it rain (oh dear, that looks rather pathetic on paper) when our nearly 18-year-old daughter stalked past and gave us the "not doing things right" look. It communicated—quite powerfully, I might add—"When I am a mom, I will never tell my teenage daughter she can't go and hang with her friends, but she's welcome to join us in the garage, talk for a few minutes, and watch it rain. I'm going to do things right." In all likelihood, Kristen already has a list of things she absolutely will not do—based entirely on a list of things I have done.

Knowing what I know now, I'm almost embarrassed to realize I once thought the same way as Kristen. But I did. So did you, perhaps.

We were the ones who fairly shouted upon confirmation of our first foray into motherhood, "It's about time I get to show these other women how it's done right." (Humility, as you can see, can be in as short supply for young mothers as our ability to hold down our breakfast during those first few weeks after conception.)

What I've Done Right

Buying my daughter a horse and letting her be a tomboy just like I was.

—Nancy, age 48

How did we know what it meant to do motherhood right?

Partly, as we've said, we just assumed we'd do the opposite of what our moms did. But also—this is true for most women I know of my generation—we learned from the experts.

You know who I mean.

I'm talking about Dr. Mom and Penelope Leach and Dr. Phil and T. Berry Brazelton (my personal favorites) and any number of other parenting gurus. I'm talking about television talk shows and newspaper columns and magazine articles. And your doctors and your friends and other people you talk to. Most moms I know are voracious consumers of parenting advice, and we started reading up on these things from the moment of conception—or perhaps much earlier. We picked our favorites and figured out our point of view. I even know some women—less rebellious than me—who put their own mothers in the expert category and struggle all their lives to lives up to the "perfect" job their own moms did.

Between Right and Reality

Whatever expert we consulted—and I consulted most of them—their advice sounded so wonderful, so sensible, so doable, so...right. All we had to do was follow their advice and their good examples and stick to our own best intentions.

The trouble is...we didn't. At least not all the time. In so many areas of motherhood, our best intentions got sidetracked in the interest of convenience or fatigue or financial difficulty or just plain reality.

So the mom who vowed to breast-feed for at least six months gives up after two months of cracked nipples and breast pumps.

The mom who would serve hot, nutritious family meals every night ends up in the fast-food drive-through on the way to dance class or T-ball practice.

The mom who envisioned maintaining a welcoming, nurturing home environment looks around at the piles of toys, clothes, old magazines, and half-completed crafts projects and bursts into tears.

The moms, like me, who swore we'd do better than our mothers did realize that 1) we're making the same mistakes our mothers made, and 2) we've come up with our own highly creative variations.

And that's when we find ourselves in the rocky foothills of Wasgonnabe, the first stop for most of us in Guiltmore.

It's actually not a steep climb—in fact, it's one of the more doable in the park because a lot of our failed expectations turn out to be false or unimportant anyway. (You may already be discovering that simple real-world experience takes care of a fair amount of this kind of guilt.) But hiking the Wasgonnabes can be tricky matter because of the uneven trails—they're full of little chinks and great big guilty gaps between the mothers we planned to be and the mothers we actually (ouch) became.

At this juncture, Sherpa Mom gently reminds fellow climbers that the first step in climbing any mountain is the easiest step. So double-check the condition of your hiking boots, safely secure your climbing gear (the terrain gets lots steeper after here), and tighten yet again the rope that secures us one to the other.

Never forget the cardinal rule of our time together: Our success resides in our remaining securely tethered to one another—for encouragement, strength, and a possible "kick in the pants" admonishment or two—roped together by our shared disappointments and achievements, our laughter and our tears.

And oh, yeah, by our guilt as well.

The Mountain in the Distance

Before we proceed too far, however, I'd like to put in a few words about where we're going. Ahead of us are the massive crags of Mt. Shoulda, the tricky ascent over Mt. Coulda, the friendlier slopes of Mt. Woulda (that one is full of handholds). There's also the treacherous trail over Mt. Inconsistency and the dark, forbidding heights of Mt. Unimaginable. But beyond them all is a pristine, snow-covered peak that gleams like Mt. Fuji in the distance. You can see it quite clearly from here in the Wasgonnabe hills.

It's beautiful.

It's inspiring.

Its slopes are smooth and inviting.

And you're never going to climb it.

That's because the highest mountain in Guiltmore—we sherpas know it as Mt. Immaculate Perfection—is really a mirage. You can't climb it because, for us humans, it doesn't exist. Its shimmering peaks are created by our own unrealistic, perfectionist expectations—the same ones that brought us here to the Wasgonnabe region. But unlike the Wasgonnabes, this mountain will always remain inaccessible, eternally beyond our reach.

The truth is, perfect mothering is simply impossible. The perfect mother does not exist. And you knew that theoretically, of course. But here in the hills of Wasgonnabe, our imperfection is as real as the rocks on the trail. And the best way to move past Wasgonnabe is to get a few basic facts straight.

First, every mom makes mistakes in the process of raising her children. Usually a lot of mistakes—little ones and big ones.

Sometimes we don't know any better.

Sometimes we're tripped up by our own past and our own pain.

Sometimes we're overtired and overstressed.

And sometimes—let's face it—we're just thoughtless or selfish or lazy. Remember what the Bible says about "All have sinned and fall short of the glory of God"? Well, this may come as a shock, but moms are sinners too.

So if you feel as if you've failed or screwed up as a mom—well, chances are you probably have. But remember, you've done a lot of things right as well. Which brings us to the second fact: Most kids really do grow up and turn out all right. Sometimes they make it because of what we've done right. Often they do so in spite of what we do wrong. Always it's because of God's unending grace.

Which is why the goal of this expedition is the lovely, peaceful valley I like to call Graceland. Before long you'll see it shimmering in the distance too—and it's three times as beautiful as Immaculate Perfection. It's the kind of place a family can really live.

So are you ready to proceed? Grab your walking stick. It's time to head onward. And upward—and over!

5

Mt. Shoulda

Things We Wish We'd Done

◎

When I tell you we're in this climb through Guiltmore's peaks together, I mean it.

While writing these chapters, I've been referencing hundreds of surveys I collected from moms, daughters, and moms-in-waiting over the course of an 18-month speaking schedule. Regardless of the subject for the weekend, I always took a portion of time during the keynote address and requested the women in attendance to fill out the form which was included in their conference packet. More specifically, I asked them to take the survey back to their hotel room and fill it out sometime during the evening when they were not as pressed for time or as apt perhaps to slap down a response without much thought. Here's how the survey read:

> Hey, ladies! Thanks for taking the time to read over this page (front and back) and giving me the priceless gift of your thoughts and opinions. I'm compiling research for an upcoming book regarding the subject of motherhood and guilt. Sigh. Can you relate? Well, since you've had a mom or perhaps are one yourself, I'm thinking you can. Simply read and answer as you'd like. I would like to use some of your comments in the aforementioned

book—please sign your name and date if I have your permission to do so. I won't use your full name, and I can give even give you a snazzy aka if you prefer. Simply make a note on the survey, and I'll honor it. Your words will help shape my writing into a work that speaks to *all* women and mothers rather than one molded simply by my lone treks through mothering guilt. Thank you for trusting me with your heart and stories.

The responses I received were magnificent! And I'm honored that these women trusted me enough to tell me the good, the bad, and the ugly regarding their experiences with mothering guilt.

It is not easy admitting you don't have it all together—as a mom or as a woman. And despite our generational fixation with reality this and reality that, sometimes we (as well as those we know and love) don't want to acknowledge our very real parenting pathologies.

I, however, am not one of those people.

I am all about getting things out in the open, dealing with things the way they are, and trying to bring honest relief to the hearts and minds of frazzled, stressed, frustrated moms everywhere…not to mention directing them to the One who can address all our collective issues.

Revealing our guilty commonalities will ultimately lead us safely to those promised vistas of Graceland. And this first jagged peak is one many of us can relate to. It's the mountain of failure, of regret. The mountain of everything we look back on and realize that we've done wrong (or think we may have done wrong) and that we've failed to do right. It's also the mountain of present-tense worries over the choices we face:

- What is the right thing to do?
- How can I help my family most?
- How can I avoid harming the people I love most?

- How can I please others and take care of myself as well?

We need to recognize right at the beginning that though the shouldas are powerful and often painful, they're not always true. In fact, this particular mountain seems to be made up of equal parts true guilt and false guilt—because most of us derive our shouldas from a variety of sources, both reliable and unreliable. (See "Who Says Thou Shalt?" on pages 78-81.)

Here are just a few of the shoulda worries that the moms I know struggle with.

Shoulda Prayed More

Consider the following: a 60-something mother visits her 39-year-old daughter, who is currently serving a 10-year prison term in one of America's most infamous penitentiaries. Her daughter now lives with convicted murderers, child abusers, and drug dealers; she is allowed only one visitor per week; and she sobs each and every time her mother presses her hand against the Plexiglas and says, "I love you."

One Friday, after a particularly difficult visit, the mother is convinced by a few well-meaning friends to attend a local women's retreat. "Come on," they tell her. "It'll do you good."

So she goes.

Planting her body in the row farthest from the main stage, she attempts to hold her emotions in check. The crowd sings praise songs about God's faithfulness and goodness. If you were to ask her, at that very moment, she'd tell you she was having a hard time believing in either.

Her mind goes back to 1967 when she stood beside her beaming husband and held her infant daughter before a large, loving church congregation. At that moment, she and her husband desired more than anything to dedicate their daughter's life to God. They spoke solemn words. They made promises.

Frame after frame of memories crowd into her mind. Her daughter proudly singing "Jesus Loves Me" to the delight of the same congregation a few years later. Her daughter saying bedtime prayers and thanking God for her mommy. Her daughter knocking on her bedroom door late one night and telling her she wanted to become a Christian. Her daughter asking difficult questions and both of them enjoying animated conversations (debate?) about the Bible and spiritual truths.

Image after image cycle through her mind in a continuous loop as the main speaker is introduced and takes the stage. The mother tries to follow the speech but finds her mind wandering back to the hollow sound of a cold steel prison door separating her from her baby girl.

Forty-five minutes pass, and then the speaker closes her talk with this story:

"Ladies, I've had countless women and mothers ask me over the years how I managed to raise four healthy, successful, and God-honoring children. Well, this is what I tell them: I prayed for my children.

"I prayed for them before they were ever born—even when I was still yet a child. I prayed for them the moment I knew I was pregnant. I prayed for them the moment they came into this world. I prayed, prayed, prayed. In fact, every night while they lived at home, I would tuck them into bed, kiss them goodnight, close their bedroom door, and then sit in the hallway and pray for them.

"Every night I prayed.

"Every night I prayed for each child.

"Every night I prayed without fail.

"You see, the Bible tells us the effective prayer of a righteous person gets results. That's how you and I can both succeed in raising healthy, successful, and God-honoring children."

And somewhere back in the farthest row a mother begins to weep.

"That's what I didn't do," she would later tell me. "I didn't pray for my daughter *every* night out in the hallway of our home. I should have prayed more."

I should have prayed more.

Am I the only one whose heart nearly wrenches loose from its moorings when considering the words of this guilt-ridden mother?

Am I the only one sorely tempted to body-slam Christian speakers (in the spirit of Christian love, of course) who espouse such guilt-inducing and theologically shaky verbiage?

I absolutely believe prayer is important. A vital thing for mothers to do. But come on! If there were a magical *number* (this being the operative word) of prayers that guaranteed successful parental outcomes, don't you think God would have communicated something about that to us? Don't you think He might have mentioned it somewhere in the Bible? Maybe a verse in the Upper Room Discourse that reads as follows: "If you'll pray for anything in my name 33 times, I will do it"?

Is this the way God works?

Does He withhold good things from us and let loose with the bad because we only managed to hit prayer number 32 on too many days or nights of our children's lives? Are our parenting problems and heartaches caused by our failure to get God's attention? Is the success or failure (real or perceived) of a child incumbent upon a right or wrong prayer—a right or wrong parental plea for wisdom or help? Even more to the point, is the weight of our children's choices or their success or failure in life our responsibility alone?

Um, no. No to every rhetorical question I've listed.

No, no, no, no, no. And just in case I wasn't clear enough, let me pose this hypothetical question yet again: If there is a lucky Lotto number of *more* praying that will guarantee our children's physical, mental, sexual, intellectual, spiritual, and social well-being…what is that number specifically?

Two times more?

Two hundred times more?

Two hundred thousand times more?

I realize I may be coming across a bit intense, but please hear me out because I know how this concept can slowly decimate a woman's confidence as a mother as well as her peaceful confidence in God.

Let me give you an example of the twisted power of "shoulda prayed more" thinking.

What I've Done Right

Instilling a love of reading in all four of my children.

—Debbie, age 37

Several summers back, newspapers reported a rash of shark attacks in various shoreline places. Children and adults went into the water and…well, they didn't come back. Now, I live in rural Illinois, and the nearest my children usually come to a body of water is the Galesburg Water Park. But that didn't keep me from thinking, *Shark attacks? Oh my, I don't think I've ever asked God to protect my children from shark attacks. I need to do that right now.*

And for those of you shaking your head mumbling, "Oh come on—really?" Yes, I did think this very thing. Crazy, huh?

Yes, it is—when you consider the fact that I have probably spoken a gazillion prayers on behalf of my children over the course of their lives. I had asked for God to protect them as they were being formed deep within my body, as they took in and then released their first deep gasps of air, as they slept, as they attended school, and as they interacted in a million different ways in the world around them. I've prayed many times for each one of them.

I've prayed broadly: God, keep them healthy. God, protect them from danger. God, help them make good choices.

I've prayed specifically: God, please stop the horrible bleeding of Ricky's head wound! God, help me find Kristen right now! God, please don't let Patrick die during this asthma attack!

All those prayers, all those specifics—and yet a part of me truly believed I'd better make a least one more specific request of God just to be sure. Now, however, I believe I had already prayed all the prayers I needed. Yet for some odd, insecure reason, a part of me irrationally reasoned that *should* my children encounter a great white, it would be in part because I *shoulda* prayed more and simply didn't get that one possible eventuality covered.

Yeesh, is there any doubt I have issues?

And so I ask myself, have I prayed these many prayers for and over my children because I believe God ultimately is in control…or in order that I might somehow (as impossible as it really is) control God?

Staring at the screen, thinking…

Still thinking…

(I'll have to get back to you on this one.)

Shoulda Stayed Home

Ah, yes, where would motherhood be without this obtrusive peak jutting out from Mt. Shoulda's skyline? And we may as well mention its twin, Shoulda Gone Back to Work, because rarely are the two separated when mothers face the age-old guilt that comes with balancing work, home, and children.

For every mom who just knew she wanted to stay home, dozens of other moms scoured every resource they could find on the subject, asked a million questions of a million people, and still felt unsure about their choice, even as they read *Love You Forever* for the sixteenth time in two hours.

For every mom who just knew she wanted to continue working part- or full-time, dozens of other moms weighed every pro and con, asked a million questions of a million people, and still wondered if they had made the right decision even as they completed an overdue work project (a book, perhaps?) and hurried to make it home in time to read *Love You Forever* for the sixteenth time that week.

The guilt of this two-pronged shoulda often follows mothers to the grave. One woman wrote this in her survey:

> My oldest son is turning 34 this year, and we have a marvelous relationship. He's grown up to be a thoughtful man, and I'm so proud of him. But there are still days, even now at age 60, when I wonder if I made a mistake by working outside our home and leaving him to watch his younger siblings when he was so young himself.

Another wrote,

> I will turn 84 years old in another month, and one of the things I've felt most guilty about as a mother is the fact that there were no jobs I could work at as a young mother, and my children had to go without so many basic things as a result of us having very little money. I just never had any other options.

Does any other topic stir the maternal water more than a good old-fashioned discussion about staying home or working outside the home? I don't think so. It's always confounded me how other women—other mothers!—have often been the first to line up and sound off regarding the individual choice each one of us has to make regarding this weighty mothering matter.

I suppose it's because this subject pokes and prods the most elemental emotions of being a mother.

We love our children.

We want our children to know they are loved.

And to have our motives or the wisdom of our choices about work called into question is to have that love challenged, held suspect. That is the last thing I want to do as I write about Mt. Shoulda. As I sit here in my living room, working on a cranky laptop, the first fact I want to acknowledge is that I don't know the details that have shaped your choice to remain home or work outside of it. I honestly don't know what you shoulda done! More to the point, if your children are still school-age and the issue is still current, I'm not prepared to state definitively what you should do now.

Rather than presenting another clichéd list of stay-at-home versus work-full-time pros and cons—which really isn't the point of this book—I'd like you to consider a few questions that speak to the underlying worry, guilt, and—this one is important—fear that are often overlooked during an argumentative discourse of the subject.

I'm assuming that all of you reading these pages love your children passionately. If you didn't love them so much, this entire issue would generate a lot less discomfort.

But you do love them. You do care about what is in their best interests. You do worry that your choices will in some way harm them. And regardless of your choice, chances are you feel some doubt and some guilt about it.

So instead of hashing over tired statistics and making recommendations that may or may not apply, I'd like you to answer the questions on pages 62-63. (Similar questions could apply to the issue of homeschooling versus private schools versus public schools.)

Take your time and ruminate on your responses for a spell. When you've done that, I believe you'll realize several things about this tricky shoulda.

Shoulda Stayed Home
Some Questions for Working Moms

1. Are you comfortable with the number of hours you're working?

2. Are you taking good care of yourself?

3. Are you working more because of what others think or because this is really the best choice for you and your family?

4. Are you making yourself and your family crazy by trying to do too many things? (Name two responsibilities you could hand over or let go of in order to find a bit more balance.)

5. Do you (will you) ask for help? Have you considered hiring a housekeeper if you can afford one? Or do you believe hiring someone means you're admitting you just can't do it all—or do it well?

6. Are you comfortable with your child-care arrangements?

7. Have you missed a lot of important family events because of work responsibilities or work-related travel?

8. Do you sense that your children are basically well-adjusted?

9. Are you connecting emotionally with your kids when you are home?

10. Are you happy or unhappy with your job in general?

11. Is your spouse or extended family supportive of your job? Do you find yourself defending your choice to them?

12. Have you doled out household responsibilities to your children (as appropriate), your spouse, or other family members living with you?

13. In what ways does your paycheck contribute to your family's budget? Are you forgetting just how valuable those contributions are?

14. Do you allow enough time to take care of morning details and evening roundups with your children at a reasonable and relaxed pace? If not, can you work toward that even today?

15. Is working outside the home the best choice for you and your family? If not, how can you change the situation either now or in the future?

Shoulda Gone Back to Work
Some Questions for Stay-at-Home Moms

1. Do you try and do *everything* in the home because you are a stay-at-home mom?

2. Has anyone told you you're wasting your college education or work potential by remaining home? What is your response?

3. Do you harbor any resentment for being a stay-at-home mom? How does that resentment express itself?

4. In general, are you enjoying your children? Do they enjoy you?

5. Do you feel important and valued by your spouse and children?

6. Do you respect yourself in the role of stay-at-home mom?

7. Are you maintaining friendships and adult relationships during this time at home?

8. Do you value your own need for stimulating conversation and mental sharpening through reading, discussion groups, or other forms of learning?

9. What do you miss about working—if you did so before staying home?

10. Are you able to find time away from the children during the day or week?

11. Are you having fun with your children?

12. Are you having fun with your husband or friends?

13. What are you providing as a stay-at-home mom that your missed paycheck cannot provide?

14. What is one specific thing you enjoy doing with your child or children that you could not do if you worked outside the home? (Be sure to do it within the week!)

15. Have you ever listed the contributions you are making to your spouse, your children, your home, your community, and your church as a stay-at-home mom? If not, why not start a list right now?

16. Is this the best choice for you and your family? If so, relax and enjoy!

As you consider the questions on the previous pages I predict that one of several possibilities will be true:

- You may realize with confidence that, given your circumstances, you've made absolutely the right child-care choice for your family.

- You may realize you've made basically the right choice, but you might need to tweak some details, such as adjusting your work hours, changing jobs, or finding a way to get out of the house a little more.

- You may face the reality that your current arrangement isn't working and you need to make some major changes.

- You may realize that your children are grown anyway and it's time you put this issue behind you.

Regardless of your response, I hope you'll admit that even though everything may not be perfect, you're still doing a pretty good job of mothering your children. I hope that instead of judging other moms who have made different decisions for their families, you'll also be inspired to give other moms a break and lay a little less guilt on everybody.

Which, by the way, leads us to our next shoulda....

Shoulda Been Easier on Other Moms

Can you remember the first mom you secretly raked over the coals? Maybe you discussed her with your husband or brought her to the attention of a few of your closest friends. Or maybe you simply watched from the fresh-meat section of a Wal-Mart SuperCenter while she had her mental breakdown near the frozen pizza.

I can tell you exactly where I was the first time it happened to me.

It was 1988, and Kristen was a mere two weeks old. At birth she had weighed in at seven pounds, three ounces, but since then she had lost nearly six ounces as I attempted to breast-feed her.

My chest stuck out like twin peaks, and they threatened to erupt at any minute.

My back hurt from all the gymnastics required to get her to latch on.

I hadn't taken a real shower (one over two minutes long) since the day of her delivery.

I was wiped out and just about to have my own mental break-down in the lobby of my pediatrician's office when the other mom walked in.

Old.

Sloppy.

Whiny and rude.

"I want to know why I haven't gotten a call back from this office concerning my son's throat culture," she barked at the receptionist. "He's been at home feeling miserable, which makes us all feel miserable, and the over-the-counter pain medication hasn't done a bit of good, and you'd think you people could get a little more organized and call a mother back with the results after the fifth time she'd called to ask…"

I couldn't believe how this mom was talking. That poor receptionist didn't stand a chance! That mom sounded to me as if she expected the entire world to stop (or call) at her command. I scanned her attire: ratty cotton leggings, a well-worn T-shirt, and—gasp— unmatched socks above her beat-up tennis shoes.

Good grief, I thought to myself, this mother really should get her act together.

The longer she stood there—glaring down the front help and demanding results—the more I began to dislike her. And the more

I thought (you know what's coming), "I will never act like that as a mother—never."

Well, I think a couple of you may have seen me at Dr. Peachey's office not so many years later as a similar scene played out. There I was in all my ratty sweats, well-worn Johnny Bravo T-shirt, and unmatched socks glory. And I was going on about something important regarding my son's health.

Sigh.

What I've Done Right

Raising my kids to take care of themselves.

—Crickett, age 50

I had an epiphany (*not* to be confused with an episiotomy) at Dr. Peachey's that morning and saw with absolute clarity the judgment and harshness of my own heart those many years before.

Sometimes a girl's got to wonder—who needs enemies when you've got other mothers?

More to the point, what does this story about my own judgmental attitude have to do with guilt? Simply that the way we judge others is closely related to the way we judge ourselves—and it's often far harsher than God's judgment of us.

And the more charity and understanding we can muster for other moms, the less guilty we'll feel.

Shoulda Disciplined Differently

I believe that discipline is an important mothering task. I really do. I'm convinced that the purposeful and controlled administration of discipline helps a child change impulsive, random behavior into controlled, purposeful behavior. I also believe such discipline should be reinforced with teaching, firmness, and reminders (without nagging).

Is that the way I disciplined my children? As I've already hinted, during my first six years of motherhood, the answer is a very regretful no. You can read all about the ups and downs, the regrets and restoration, in *She's Gonna Blow!,* but for the sake of discussion let me simply state that I could cite dozens and dozens of angry-mom shouldas related to this topic.

- I shoulda been more patient.
- I shoulda thought more about what I was doing.
- I shoulda studied my children better and adjusted my discipline accordingly.
- I shoulda *never* struck my children in anger.
- I shoulda asked for help.
- I shoulda relaxed more and made allowances for mistakes (theirs and mine).
- I shoulda distinguished between childishness and rebellion much earlier in their lives.
- I shoulda been less worried about what my family and friends thought of my mothering.

My mail and the feedback from my speaking tells me that many other moms have legitimately messed up when disciplining their kids. We went too far with our words or our screaming or our threats or the physical actions we referred to as "spankings" or "whippings." Now we find ourselves a bit farther down the trail, and looking back always seems to bring regret, guilt, and shame.

But being too strict or harsh is not the only kind of discipline shoulda that moms encounter. I have also heard from multitudes of women who feel guilt over being too lax about discipline. Their shoulda guilt wasn't about the way they administered physical discipline. Rather, they wonder if they taught their children to practice self-discipline as they grew older.

For example, a woman named Ava wrote this:

> I look at my adult children, ages 27, 24, and 22, and it seems as though none of them really know how to stick with anything. The oldest has yet to hold a job for longer than 24 months. He is married with two children of his own, but he doesn't seem to be involved as a father in their day-to-day lives. My middle child, a girl, dropped out of college (which her father and I had paid for up to that point) the fall of her senior year because she just "didn't feel like she wanted to pursue her degree." We told her we "just didn't feel" like carrying the balance of her student loan and told her we expected her to get a job and start repayment. We're still waiting. And our youngest, well, I'll be honest with you, I was just plain tired after he was born, and I let a lot of things slip through the cracks. So I'm not surprised he's like he is. But my other two? Well, in hindsight I guess I should have done things a lot differently when it comes to teaching and demanding discipline from them.

Perhaps you have been in the same place as Ava—looking back years or just a few months and wondering what it was you missed. Wondering what specific detail or example or teaching moment you didn't take advantage of, what values you failed to pass on to your child.

One mother told me about the discipline problems she was currently engaged in with her teenage daughter. The girl disregarded curfews, and the mother suspected she was slipping out of the house in the wee hours of the night. In fact, she had begun to pray quite specifically that she would be able to catch her daughter in the act. (Now, that's a prayer I can relate to!) She kept an ear and eye out. And sure enough, one early morning the daughter crept back through her bedroom window to discover both her mother and father sitting on her down-filled comforter. Busted!

Now, Mom assumed her daughter would be as taken aback by their presence as they had been when they found what she had been doing. (First rule of mothering: Assume nothing.) But the daughter didn't seem all that concerned. When they questioned her behavior, in fact, she replied, "Well, you could have called me on my cell phone."

(Grr...hold me back. This is the sort of thing that still tends to bring out my residual angry-mom propensities.)

Shaking her head with an oh-so-familiar-to-me hint of resignation, the mother looked to her husband and sighed, "Well, I guess we shoulda disciplined her better regarding proper sneaky teenage behavior."

Too much discipline, too little discipline, the wrong kind of discipline—almost all of us have our specific regrets. But hear me, moms! We can't possibly cover all the bases of discipline as well as we'd like to. What works with one child won't work with another. What succeeds one day may fail the next. Something is always going to slip by. And that's not to mention the fact that our children have their own minds and make their own decisions, complicating our efforts at discipline.

So yes, we should examine ourselves and work on correcting lazy behavior or ill-tempered leadership. Yes, we need to seek a peaceful, settled place of nurturing where the entire weight of our children's world does not rest on our weak and fallible shoulders.

But no matter how we try, we're still going to have to find a way to move past this particular outcropping of Mt. Shoulda, to make peace with our disciplining mistakes and all our other accumulated mothering guilt. (You'll find guidance to doing just that in an upcoming chapter.)

Shoulda Appreciated My Mom More

As I've already mentioned, I entered motherhood with the serene confidence that I would do it much better than my mom did. But let me tell you, as soon as reality struck (read: as soon as I had been in the mommy trenches for more than two years) I began to revaluate some of those thoughts. As I took on the role of mother, I began to see with a bit more clarity why she had done the things she had done and said the things she said. And now, many years later, I understand even better.

I understand why she insisted I make my bed every single morning of my life.

I understand why she asked me where I was going, who I was going to be with, and what I was going to be doing.

I understand how much control it must have taken her to not fall apart the August day I hugged her and Dad goodbye at college.

For many of us, this particular shoulda is one of the most poignant guilt sources in our lives. Most of us are old enough and have experienced enough foul-ups as mothers to recognize the incredibly good jobs our mothers did when facing situations similar to those we now face. And this recognition can be a source of regret—especially if we've never gotten around to telling our moms how much we have come to appreciate them.

I asked women at my seminars to tell me what their mothers did right and whether they had ever thanked them. Of the hundreds of responses I received, only five were from women who could not tell me anything good about their moms. The rest filled their surveys with touching memories and glowing descriptions colored by the guilt of not appreciating their moms enough:

> My mother always let me know I was loved—she showed it physically, and she said it verbally. My mom sang songs about Jesus, and I remember her doing just that as she cleaned up my scraped knees after I fell off my bicycle…I'm not sure she realizes how much she did right. I think I should probably tell her.

> My mom was always sooooo…protective of me when I was growing up. After seeing firsthand how scary it really is in the real world, I am grateful for her protection. It was the right thing to do, and I've told her that a hundred times.

> I was two weeks old the first day I went to church. My mother's faithfulness to Jesus Christ remained unfailing to the day she died. She taught me the value of standing firm in all circumstances and putting God first, my family second, and all the other stuff as it came along. I was able to tell my mother all these things while she was alive—not at her funeral—and that's one more thing we did right.

The best thing about this particular shoulda is that it's relatively easy to conquer, especially if your mother is still living. You don't even have to wait until you get to the "solution" part of this book. In fact, I suggest that you turn this book over right now and pick up the phone or fire up the computer or pull out your stationery. Let her know right now how much you've come to appreciate her. Tell her exactly what she did right as a mom! Even better, plan a special trip home and tell her face-to-face.

A friend of mine did just that.

She traveled home unexpectedly, took her mother out for a delicious meal, and then read to her a two-page list of "What You Did Right" thoughts and memories. They were both a blubbering mess before she ever made it to item number five. And that's one particular guilty shoulda she's crossed off her list entirely now.

I can't guarantee that your solution will be so simple. Your mother may no longer be alive. Illness or dementia or some other difficulty could prevent you from communicating clearly. You may have come to appreciate your mom better, but your relationship is still strained. But even if you can't express appreciation directly to your mom, I recommend that you sit down and write out your thoughts. You could also share them with a friend, a sibling, your spouse, your pastor. Take the time to specifically thank God for your mom and ask forgiveness for your lack of gratitude and appreciation. You might even want to write out a list of things your mom did for you that you would like to do with your own children.

After all, imitation may be the sincerest form of flattery.

It's also a great way to say thank you…and to lighten the load of guilt in your life.

Shoulda Appreciated Each Stage of Childhood More

I think the test stick had just turned blue confirming my first pregnancy when I said aloud to my husband, "Oh, I can't wait to feel the baby kick!"

That's *so* me—to fixate on what is just around the corner instead of enjoying what I have right in front of me. Not that there's anything intrinsically wrong with a mother longing to feel her baby's first kick. Or looking forward to any of the milestones in her children's lives: holding their head up without looking like a bobble-head, rolling over, eating solid foods, speaking their first words, learning to crawl and walk, going off to school, graduating, and even raising children of their own.

What I've Done Right

I tried to always make a point to cook my son and daughter's favorite dessert when they returned home from college breaks. I still do when they return home with their own families.

—Ida, age 63

It's natural and good for a mother to look forward eagerly to the next phase. However, I've found in my own life that when I allow myself to obsess over the milestone yet to come, I can grow disgruntled or even resentful about where my children are now. Other mothers have shared with me similar feelings.

I have four children, and I can honestly tell you that I didn't spend near enough time enjoying the baby stage of number two and number three. Maybe it's a given with the middle children in a family, but when I look back, most of my memories are made up of wishing they'd get out of the diaper stage sooner. It seemed like I was changing diapers every six minutes. Sigh. Now my "babies" are 17 and 19. I really should have not rushed their growing up so much.

I couldn't wait until my only child got through her teen years! I dreaded every morning, every afternoon, and every night of those hormonal ups and downs. My husband would tell me, "Mary, someday you're going to wish you had mellowed out a bit and simply enjoyed this time the best you could." I thought he was crazy. Turns out I do feel guilty about wishing away all that time. My daughter is married and has a three-year-old daughter of her own. And I bet you can guess what I tell her to do: Enjoy that child at every stage of her life!

Is there a particular stage of your children's lives that you've found yourself wishing away—or at the very least, hurrying along?

With my firstborn, Kristen, I was often driven by a crazy first-time-mom desire to see her accomplish new and exciting things. I remember living in Greenville, Mississippi, just a few months after she was born and taking picture after picture of her lying on her belly, wobbling her head around as she tried to hold it upright, and sticking her tongue out. Then I would pack her up, drive to the mall near Wal-Mart, and take my film to the one-hour photo lab. This was long before the days of digital cameras and inexpensive developing, so I easily spent $12 or $14 per roll for the one-hour service. But I didn't care. All I wanted was photographic proof of Miss Kristen making her way through yet another baby milestone.

My behavior continued until Ricky Neal came on the scene. Kristen was not quite 19 months old when this nine-pound, eight-ounce bundle of boy power began making his presence known in our family. Before long I was capturing photos of Ricky Neal being mauled by his sister. And that's when I began wishing away Kristen's toddler years and counting down the days until Ricky Neal could at least sit up and defend himself against her zealous acts of sisterly love. (There were a lot of photographs of Ricky Neal sitting in a playpen, safe from his sister's advances.)

As the years passed and my children grew, I still tended to wish away the present—but for a different reason. Those were my angry years, and during some of my worst *She's Gonna Blow!* moments, I wished myself out of my children's lives entirely. I was so ashamed of the mother I had turned out to be and so full of guilt over behaviors and attitudes I knew were destructive to my heart, my home, and my children that I just wanted to put the whole situation behind me.

It wasn't until I got a few peeks of those promised vistas of Grace-land (thanks to implementing simple but specific strategies for taking back my brain as a mom plus seeking medical and spiritual counsel for depression and dealing with the past) that I was able to live—I mean truly live—in the present. Only then did I begin to really enjoy my children's lives, their personalities, their abilities, and their presence in my own life. But I still had a tendency to live in the future and forget to appreciate the present. In fact, I still struggle to maintain an attitude of present-day contentment on my own. What has helped me most is an ongoing friendship with another mom who is willing to listen and to firmly remind me of the blessing of each day, month, and year I had with my children.

How about you? Do you ever find yourself wishing away a particular stage in your child's life and longing for the future? Maybe you find yourself thinking thoughts like these:

- I can't wait until this baby gets old enough to sleep through the night.

- I can't wait until this toddler learns how to control his emotions in public.

- I can't wait until this junior-high kid understands math better than I do.

- I can't wait until this 11-year-old calms down emotionally and quits eating so much.

- I can't wait until this teenager moves out of the house.

- I can't wait until I'm through being a mother.

Ah, but you and I both know we are never through being mothers. Not really. I'm 40 years old, and just the other day my 75-year-old mom called to remind me to set my clocks forward for daylight savings time. She still wants me to call and let her know when I make it home safely when traveling back from my hometown. And she will still float me a little cash when I find myself in a tight spot.

Now, I imagine Mom wished more than a few times while I was growing up that I would be better with remembering details, calling and letting her know where I was and if I was okay, and handling my finances with the excellent acuity she and my father have practiced for nearly 50 years of marriage.

She probably sighed with relief the day I got married. But she never signed off as my mom. And neither will you or I.

So here's what I'd like us to do, ladies. Let's acknowledge the "hurry up and grow up" wishing we're tossing about in our hearts and heads. It doesn't mean that we're bad moms or that we don't love our children…it's simply one of the slopes of Mt. Shoulda with which we need to contend. And the best way to deal with this particular shoulda is with truth and gratitude. We need to face the reality of what we are thinking and then deliberately give thanks for the circumstances and situations we are currently wishing away.

Yes, that's what I said: Get real and give thanks. (Hey! Hey! Don't even think of skipping this part of the chapter.) This is one of those "speak truth" realities I have hammered home in every book I've written because I believe with all my heart, mind, and soul that the only way our heart, mind, and soul are going to deal effectively with guilt, fear, anger, worry, yada, yada, yada, is through the power of truth—biblical and practical. I'm also firmly convinced that at the heart of just about every biblical and practical truth we might have to face is the reality that God is present in whatever is going on in our lives—loving and caring for us even when we can't detect His presence.

So speak out loud the "hurry up" you're wishing for. You might want to tell your husband or maybe one of those wonderful women in your life who are willing to help you find your way off this peak. Say it and then speak practical and spiritual truth regarding it. Then face the truth of God's presence in your life by saying thank You.

Let me give you an example. Let's say you're wishing away those innumerable piles of clothing strewn across the floor of your teenage son's bedroom. (Not that I have any personal knowledge of such a wish. Nah, not me.) Let's say nearly every time you walk into his room (cough, cough), you say to yourself, "I can't wait till this kid has to take care of his own laundry and I don't."

You've got a legitimate gripe, by the way. And yes, he really should pick up his clothes, throw them in the clothes hamper, and hang up his clean jeans and shirts uniformly in his clothes closet—*without* needing to be told. But in some of our mother worlds the probability of that actually happening is slim to none. And yes, it would be nice to hear him say one day (like tomorrow!), "Gee, Mom, I have seen the error of my ways and simply want to acknowledge what a slob I've been. I promise to do better. In fact, from now on I'll take care of my own laundry." That's even a worthwhile disciplining goal—teaching him to be more responsible.

However, until that actually occurs you're going to have to deal with things the way they are and try and find truth for now. So here's what I would do. I'd go ahead and pick up those clothes because I refuse to send a child of mine to school wearing wrinkled, smelly clothes. As I picked up each item of clothing I would begin to speak truth and give thanks for each and every item.

See that St. Louis Cardinals T-shirt crammed underneath his bed frame? "God, I just want to say thank You for a healthy, mostly coordinated teenaged son who can play sports and enjoy watching baseball with his family."

Now I'm grabbing a couple pairs of jeans with a disgustingly dirty sock stuffed into one of the pockets. Heavy sigh...gotta think about this one for a minute. Okay, here goes: "God, I just want to tell You how much I've enjoyed watching my son grow into a six-foot-four teenager whose jeans inseam is a bigger number than my waist size. I also thank You for the money to purchase more socks."

A simplistic approach?

Maybe so.

But then again, it's not that simplistic. It's simply doable, and it works. Bit by bit, truth by simple truth, you can chip away at needless guilt by cherishing each stage of your children's lives.

And that's one more *shoulda* that won't be heaping guilt on your life.

Who Says Thou Shalt?
Some Questions to Help You Confront False Guilt

Shouldas from Your Mom

(Sometimes we respond to shouldas as if they were absolute commandments—"thou shalts" and "thou shalt nots"—without stopping to think whether they reflect our own values. You may have picked up the following "shalts" in your family of origin. They may be healthy or unhealthy, appropriate or inappropriate, and you might not even be aware of how they drive your choices—but they do. Examine them in light of what you really believe and care about—and what you want to teach your own kids.)

- Thou shalt make thy bed every day.
- Thou shalt always wear clean underwear.
- Thou shalt never talk to strangers or pick up hitchhikers.

- Thou shalt always put thy children first (even before thy husband).
- Thou shalt put thy work ahead of thy family.
- Thou shalt never stand up for thyself.
- Thou shalt always try to get thine own way.

Shouldas from Your Culture

(These "thou shalts" derive from national, ethnic, community, and church standards. You may have picked them up from other people or from the media. And they may well be appropriate, but they can also be destructive—and as you'll note, many contradict each other. Choose for yourself which ones truly matter to you, which don't, and which are worth ignoring, even though ignoring them may bring disapproval from your community.)

- Thou shalt get them before they get you.
- Thou shalt always stay busy.
- Thou shalt look out for number one.
- Thou shalt keep thy house spotless (and decorated) and thy lawn immaculate.
- Thou shalt recycle.
- Thy kids will be stunted if they don't get in the best schools.
- Thou shalt volunteer as a room mother (or soccer coach or Sunday school teacher).
- Thou shalt stay married no matter what.
- Thou shalt divorce if thou aren't happy.
- Thou shalt fulfill thyself at all cost.
- Thou shalt entertain like Martha Stewart.

- Thou shalt provide thy children with designer clothes.
- Thou shalt stimulate thy children's minds with all the latest techniques.
- Thou shalt never lose thy temper.
- Thou shalt always be a cool mom.
- Thou shalt set a good example for thy children.
- Thy children shall always be clean and presentable.
- Thou shalt drive a minivan (or SUV, or hybrid car, or pickup truck...).
- Thou shalt stay at home with kids (or homeschool).
- Thou shalt work outside the home, engage thy mind, and provide all the little extras for thy family.
- Thou shalt breast-feed.
- Thou shalt never expose thy kid to potential allergens.
- Thou shalt never take thine eyes off thy children.
- Thou shalt never be an overprotective parent.

Shouldas from God

(These are the real "thou shalts" to obey—or strive to obey. And they're really a lot simpler than many people think.)

- The Ten Commandments (Exodus 20:1–17).
- Jesus's summary of the commandments: "Thou shalt love the Lord thy God with all thy heart, and with all thy soul, and with all the strength, and with all thy mind; and thy neighbour as thyself" (Luke 10:27).
- Jesus' teachings from the Gospels, including such things as not

worrying, praying and giving in private, treating all people as if they were Jesus Himself, and forsaking all else to follow Him.

- Jesus' example from the Gospels, including making time for prayer, taking women and children seriously, respecting authority, loving family but loving God more, and following God's example of forgiving again and again.

- The New Testament's instructions about living together as God's people, such as living in harmony if possible, being careful about the tongue, not being a stumbling block, submitting to each other, enduring suffering patiently, waiting in hope for the coming of the Lord, and focusing your mind on good things.

- General biblical teachings about parenting, like training up a child, talking about God's laws with family, loving justice, and doing mercy.

6

Mt. Coulda

Things That Might Have Been

I'm writing this chapter while traveling on a Sunday afternoon to Hannibal, Missouri, wedged between my two older children (to avoid World War III) in a backseat far too small for a 40-plus woman's backside as my husband and youngest son chat away in the front. I'm attempting to finish a few needed chapters, but my mind keeps going back to the baby dedication that took place during our church service a little less than an hour ago.

Two infant girls, Katherine Rose and Kiley, snuggled in our pastor's arms as he solemnly charged the parents and church members to nurture these little ones and to instill within their hearts and lives the love and joy of Jesus Christ. I am such a softy about these things, and the fact that I had been mulling over the contents of this book for the past eight months probably made me that much mushier. It's just that watching those babies and seeing the earnest expressions on their parents' faces touched my mothering heart deeply.

I keep thinking back to that morning in 1988 when we dedicated our little Kristen at Hannibal Baptist Fellowship. I remember the carefully chosen outfit I dressed her in. I remember the proud smiling faces of our family and friends. And more than anything else I remember how incredibly hopeful life seemed at that moment. I felt I could do anything as a mom, and I couldn't begin to fathom a time when I might believe otherwise.

Oh, the irony.

You see, while I sit here attempting to compose words and phrases and indulging in some sentimental memories, that same baby daughter—now well into her teen years—is doing her very best to maintain absolute zero contact with me. See, I snapped at her a few minutes before we left for Hannibal, and she's still mad. So she shies away from speaking to or touching me, oblivious to the poignant mix of resignation and release that fills my heart and mind.

In the last chapter I wrote passionately about the importance of telling the truth. I set myself up as someone who strives to get things out in the open. Well, now I realize that isn't completely accurate. For if I were really the truth teller I believe I am, I would turn to my daughter and say, "You should know that the reason I nearly bit your head off back home in the kitchen has nothing to do with you and everything to do with me. I came out of church thinking of all the dreams I had for you, the promises I made to myself as your young mom. I glanced at you sitting next to your father in church and saw all the things I didn't do or did wrongly, and I thought of what I could have done differently. I felt sad and more than a little disappointed with myself, and instead of owning up to those feelings, I simply made you the scapegoat for them. I'm sorry."

Now that would be getting things out in the open. That would be telling the truth.

But I didn't do that.

Instead, I did what I do all too often with those who are really, really, *really* close to me—I diverted my true feelings and masked them with something else. And for me, that "something else" usually includes but isn't limited to the following:

- creating a wall of verbal and emotional silence
- spewing verbal sarcasm (yes, rumblings of Mt. Momma!)
- taking my confusion or frustration out on my husband
- shutting down emotionally
- pretending I'm not feeling the way I am

And aren't those psychologically healthy and spiritually sensitive responses?

Oh, boy.

My friends, it looks like Sherpa Mom may have more to learn in this chapter than any of you. But that's okay. It's more than okay, really. It's what Christ had in mind when He encouraged us to bear with the failings of those who are weak and to make up what is lacking in one another's faith along the journey of life (see Romans 15:1-3).

Never doubt that Jesus knows exactly where each of us currently stands on Guiltmore's peaks. He knows. He understands. And unlike this Sherpa Mom, who despite her best intentions doesn't have it all together, He does. He's roped together with us as we trek the slopes of Mt. Coulda. And He's here with me in this crowded backseat as I ponder the coulda realities of raising our children.

What will we find on Mt. Coulda? This is the mountain where we confront our missed opportunities, all the things we could have done differently to the benefit of ourselves and our children—but didn't. Here are some possibilities.

Coulda Lightened Up

Several of the mothers who responded to my survey wished they had learned this lesson much sooner. Here are a couple of examples:

If I could do it again, I would look for the funny things of life in the day-to-day routine of waking up, getting the kids ready for school, juggling work and home, and attempting to get everything wrapped up by nine o'clock in the evening. I took myself (and the role of motherhood) far too seriously if you must know.

I realize now (22 years after the fact) I could have alleviated a lot of tension and stress between myself and my two children if I could have only learned to laugh at myself as a mom. I was always so worried that I would come across as weak or not in control if I actually laughed about mistakes and goofs I made.

Who among us hasn't at some point chosen to suck up laughter and plant a stoic expression of maternal control across our face instead? Being a naturally sanguine person, I may be less guilty of doing this than some other personality types, but I've done it nonetheless.

In particular, I remember certain family events with grandparents, aunts, uncles, and cousins four times removed, when my children decided to do something…well, stupid. You know what I'm talking about. One of those times when your children's entire genetic gene pool has gathered around them, and you want them to be models of beauty and grace good behavior—a credit to their breeding and your impeccable training.

So they belch.

Or break wind.

Or do both and fall over in hysterical peals of laughter.

And you look at their father as if to say, "Do something with *your* DNA!"

Chances are you'll throw them an icy stare, which only furthers their raucous roars. Then you'll verbally threaten with something drastic. Or physically pull on one of their ears and escort them outside where you can have a little talk.

But never, no, never, will you allow yourself to chuckle.

After all, adult mothers of children do not laugh at (condone) preposterous public behavior. Even if it *is* amusing.

Do you recall that my tell-all guilt list included the fact that all three of my children can and do quote large portions of dialogue from the *Austin Powers* movie? Well, I'll grant you it may not be the finest aspect of my mothering legacy. But truth be told, nothing makes me laugh harder than listening to Ricky Neal tell his little brother, "Oh, Scottie, tone it down a notch." And watching Patrick follow up by tweaking his fingers together and, before his brother can complete a thought, say, "Sh...um...sh." (Maybe you have to see the movie to appreciate that one.)

Anyway, I would never have laughed at such things ten or twelve years ago. I would have huffed and puffed and begun a verbal dissertation on the moral breakdown of the American family due to the influence of power-hungry movie moguls and lax parents. (Ugh.) And I suppose some of you reading these pages may believe I still should do that...and turn from my shallow-mom ways.

But the truth is, what I really feel guilty about are those years when I coulda lightened up a lot. I feel bad for Kristen and Ricky Neal, who received the brunt of my heavy-handed, humorless mothering in their early years.

What I've Done Right

Showering my children with outward expressions of love when they were little. (They get so tired of me hugging on them as teens!)

—Doreen, age 44

I really wish I knew then what I know now, which is that I didn't have to throw out my sense of humor when I became a mom. Heaven knows that was when I needed it most. I really coulda done better on this one. But again, I didn't.

Coulda Shown My Children More Physical Love

Have you ever gotten to the end of the day and realized you haven't hugged your child?

Or found yourself caught up in a mad swirl of schedules, appointments, and deadlines, only to realize you hadn't made physical contact with your spouse or children for a day or two?

Have you purposely withheld your physical touch from your children because you were mad at them or wanted to punish them for something they had said or done to hurt your feelings or disappoint you?

Have you found it difficult to show physical affection for your children? And are you embarrassed or even ashamed to admit it?

I have to tell you, this coulda reality truly hasn't been much of an issue in my life.

I can recall a time or two when I shut down emotionally as a mother and willfully chose to limit physical contact with my children. This was back in the days when I was really struggling with my anger. I feared I could actually hurt the children physically if I didn't simply draw the line and back off. So I did—but not for long.

For all my many shortcomings, I've always been a mother who loves to touch her children.

I place kisses on the top of their heads.

I pat their arms and say, "Love you." (Just like my mom did with me.)

I scratch their backs.

I rub their feet. (This takes a bit more coaxing for me to do.)

I run my fingers through their hair.

I hug them first thing in the morning, the moment I walk in the door from traveling, or as they're walking through the kitchen and happen to catch my attention.

And I really miss the days when my three could somehow find a way to sit on my lap, lie across my legs, or sprawl across my chest...all at the same time!

But not everyone can say the same.

Truth is, it's not possible for me to have personally experienced every guilty possibility available to mothers. (Thank goodness.) And I always hesitate to speak about issues I haven't experienced. But this is where the beauty of honesty and confession comes into play as an author. I don't have to know or feel everything, and I certainly don't have to make up words or stories to prove some point. All I have to do is tap into the plethora of information that real moms just like you and me have graciously allowed me to collect. And surveys indicate that many mothers had (or have) difficulty demonstrating the physical side of their love.

Perhaps that's true of you too.

It isn't that you loved your children any less. It may be simply a matter of your temperament—you're just not the touchy feely type. It may be a result of your upbringing—you were not raised to be physically demonstrative. A traumatic event in your early life may have made touch difficult for you. Or you may simply have allowed yourself to become distracted or withdrawn.

Then one day you look back with regret and realize, *I coulda shown my children more physical love.*

If you happen to be one of those moms, take heart and know you are not alone. The truth is you love your children and have probably gone to great lengths to ensure their safety, their health, and their education. You may have stayed up late at night to sew for them, arranged for wonderful opportunities, invested money for their future. All of these things bear evidence of your love—and at some level your children probably know this.

At the same time, it may be true that you missed out on the simplest and most effective way of demonstrating your love for your child.

You coulda shown your children more physical love.

You didn't.

But let me hasten to add that it's not too late—even if your children are grown and away from home. You might be surprised at the way a simple touch of the hand can sweeten your relationship. (I'll have more suggestions for adding this dimension to your life in a future chapter.)

It might feel a bit awkward. But it's better than feeling guilty and regretful. And it's better than getting stuck on this particularly cold slope of Mt. Coulda.

Coulda Managed Our Money Better

If you've read any of my previous books, you're already aware that managing money has never been my strong point. It's not my husband's greatest strength, either. And though both of us have learned a lot in the past decade or two, we're still haunted by a number of money-related couldas that tend to leave me feeling guilty and defeated.

My biggest financial coulda at the moment has to do with the looming prospect of paying college tuition for our kids—and our abysmal preparation for doing it. I've been going over banking records, credit reports and ratings, 1040 tax statements, and once-owned stock holdings, and for the life of me I cannot figure out how we have managed to come up with such meager savings for this important area of our children's lives. (And Ricky Neal is right behind her.)

Now, I know that many of you reading this book are probably saying to yourself, "Hey! I had to work and pay my way through college and deal with student loans, so what's the big deal?"

Well, it's a big deal for me. Thanks to my parents' careful management, I did not have to create debt in my life as a college student, and I did not bring debt into my marriage a few months after graduation. So for me, it has always been an important ideal (an ethereal concept) that Rick and I would provide the same opportunity for our children. I wanted to pay for our children's college tuition and not see them acquire loans that would strap them down with debt early in life. I always considered our ability to provide funds for their college work to be a gift of magnificent proportions that their father and I could and would gladly offer.

Sigh.

I thought all those thoughts during Kristen's first year of life.

I thought all those thoughts as she entered kindergarten.

I thought all those thoughts as she tackled junior high.

I thought all those thoughts as she asked me for advice regarding the high school classes she should take in preparation for college.

And I thought all those thoughts as she and I lay in her bed, talking about college applications and her hopes and dreams for her career.

I thought them, and I felt enormously guilty. Still do, in fact.

I know that in the grand scheme of things, this coulda guilt may not be as insurmountable or profound as something you are confronting on a daily basis, so please be patient with me if you're feeling annoyed or irritated. Then again, you may be struggling with the same problem or a similar one. I know I'm not the only person to struggle with finance-related guilt.

Besides, this particular guilt isn't simply about money. Well, okay… it is a *lot* about money—but not entirely. The guilt I have is more about facing my own failure, my missed opportunities to provide for my children the way I wanted. The grim reality is that I failed to consistently choose what was necessary to make my dreams happen.

I said yes to spending and no to saving far too many times.

I viewed our finances through a myopic lens rather than one that offered a broader perspective. I simply didn't realize how quickly the years would pass.

And when the time came, I came up short. In this one specific way, I have failed my daughter and myself.

Now, am I possibly being a little too hard on myself? You betcha! That's always a possibility when it comes to coulda guilt.

Truth is, Rick and I made many choices over the years that curtailed our income potential but that neither of us would go back and change. It was right for me to stay home full-time during my first 14 years as a mother. It was right for Rick to leave a potentially high-paying management career in order to reduce marital and family stress. And when I did decide to strike out as an official "working woman," I was right to choose a speaking and writing career that allowed me to be home 95 percent of the time. And though these choices came at a certain financial cost, I know (yes, really know) that they have made my family and me truly wealthy in love, relationships, unity, and a shared faith in Jesus Christ.

I know all those things…but I'm still wrestling with the guilt and the reality that neither Wheaton College nor Illinois State University will accept a check written on the Barnhill Love and Unity account.

So that's a painful coulda I'm struggling with right now.

You may be struggling with a similar one.

Perhaps you wonder if you coulda taken a second job to pay for music lessons or private-school tuition. Or squirreled away more cash for a computer. Or found a better-paying job that allowed your family to live in a better part of town.

Financially speaking, a lot of us coulda done better.

But we didn't.

Coulda Been a Better Mom

This is the biggest coulda of all, isn't it—the one that sums up all the rest. To get a better sense of how it affects the average mom, I decided to do a little online research.

I didn't visit the official parenting sites that feature expert speakers, writers, counselors, or professors. Instead I plunged into the wonderful cyberworld of estrogen-driven, lactating, loving, "I've got a story to tell you about my kids, my tilted cervix, and my mommy guilt" blogs on the Net.

Hundreds of moms are posting their observations, interactions, frustrations, wrangling, joys, fears, and more than a few baby photos online. As a result, I now know all sorts of things about families I've never actually met.

I know the color and texture of Caitlyn's first postbirth poo.

I know that Jackson and Mia ate cat food for breakfast.

I know that the blogger who calls her site *All Mothers Are Slightly Insane* has a killer sense of humor.

I also tracked the growth chart of little Carter and know more about his mother's fifth bout of mastitis than I could *ever* possibly want to know. (Pressing hands against breasts and wincing.)

Take it from me, these women have "getting things out in the open" covered. And their blogs are full of references to what they feel they need to do in order to become better moms. For example, this is what Jodi writes:

> I need to take a deep breath before I scream! I need to enjoy every moment of the kids, even the crappy ones! [And] I shouldn't let them watch so much TV—but I work at home and need to get things done!

Another mom, Debra, believes taking the time to write her blog helps make her a better mom.

I so look forward to this time every day, sitting at the computer...I don't see how this can be anything but good for my family. It's the creative me that my husband fell in love with, not the nanny/cook/housekeeper me (though he loves her too). When my imagination is engaged, I can play deep-sea explorers with my daughter and actually enjoy it. I can make up silly songs that make my infant son giggle. Taking time for me is actually giving me back to my family, and I wouldn't change things for the world.[4]

These are pretty healthy observations, wouldn't you agree? But there are others that made my facial hair stand on end! I'm not going to quote them verbatim, but I will tell you the message they conveyed in a nutshell: Being a "better" mom almost always entailed beating oneself up for something one is not—especially when compared to other mothers.

What I've Done Right

Being generous with my time.

—Nancy, age 31

This is where Mt. Coulda starts to look a lot like Mt. Shoulda. For when we compare ourselves to other mothers, it's all too easy to assume that we *should* be like them. Surely we've all had our moments (or hours or decades) when we did our mothering in the cold shadow of such self-imposed standards. I know I spent a lot of my early years huddled there. I wished I were...

as patient as Gayla,
as creative as Deanna,

as selfless as Debbie,
as tenacious as Audrey,
as financially astute as Dona,
as tenderhearted as Diana,
as hospitable as Becky,
as determined as Denise,
as calm as Rita,
as mellow as Chris,
as physically active as Lisa,
and as spiritually aware as Mary...the mother of Jesus!

Um...yes, I did have the audacity to contrast myself with the mother of God. Perhaps I should have wished for the same humility! At any rate, you probably know how well I lived up to this particular kind of wishful thinking. Regardless of my striving to be the kind of mom I thought I should be, I never made it. I always seemed to fall short of the mark.

Instead of patience, I spouted off with verbal irritation.

Instead of creativity, I stuck in another *Veggie Tales* video and told the kids to have at it.

Instead of selflessness, I thought far too much about me.

Instead of tenacity, I simply lowered a few expectations to ground zero.

Instead of financial awareness, I charged a Playskool kitchen set and could barely make the $34 minimum payment.

I think you get the idea!

I really wanted to be all those things. I really wanted to be a better mom. But I couldn't live up to my own self-imposed standards. And instead of owning up to that simple reality, I spent far too many days watching other women and feeling guilty because—I was sure—I coulda done better.

The item that many of us have deemed quintessential to better mothering is often an elusive, evasive, and...(I'm looking for an "e" word)...*exasperating* notion that can seldom be maintained for the long haul.

Here's a news flash: Better mothering will always be an unattainable summit if it is tied to comparison. Now, I am not saying we should stop examining our lives as moms and simply shoot for the lowest expectations possible. (Quite frankly, I don't think most moms could do that even if they wanted to!) What I am saying is that once again we must take back our brains and thoughtfully consider the whys and what-fors of "coulda done better" guilt.

Why do you think you need to be a better mom anyway?

Did someone come up to you and say, "You know, I've been watching you for a while, and I really think you'd be a better mom if you'd just _____" (fill in the blank)?

Did your husband or mother-in-law tell you there was something better you could be doing or saying or acting or feeling as a mom?

Or have you simply believed, for longer than you can remember not believing, that "being better" was simply something you weren't living up to?

Who are you comparing yourself to? Is it your mother? Or your mother-in-law? Perhaps a close friend from high school or a college roommate who seems out to better you in every way?

Or perhaps it's a woman you've never officially met but someone you've watched at playgroup, the grocery store, or through the living room window as you walked by her home one evening. (Oh, come on! I know I'm not the only mom who has spied into those nondraped windows and imagined what another mom's life was like. Er, I *hope* I'm not the only one!)

Regardless, we watch friend and stranger alike and come up with all sorts of ways we've missed the boat and passed up opportunities to be better.

But when we do that, aren't we missing an obvious point?

The truth is, in hindsight, we will *always* be able to think of something we coulda done better. And wish with all our heart that we'd done better. And feel guilty that we didn't do better.

But again, that's hindsight. And in this case hindsight may not even be accurate. Because the real question for most of us is this: *Could I really have done better?*

And I believe the answer for most of us, when we consider who we were at the time—and what we knew then (or didn't know) and what we had to work with—is this:

I did the best I could.

Sure, we feel the guilt. But that's what we're here for, after all—to move past the guilt.

So trek on. I'll meet you at the base of Mt. Woulda.

7

Mt. Woulda

Things We Would Tell One Another

◎

I think I can safely say that I've pretty much taken it upon myself to feel guilty about everything at some point in time as a mom.

There was the morning my 11-year-old daughter pointed out the toast crumbs dotting the landscape of the I Can't Believe It's Not Butter container. I never thought twice about taking my knife, swiping a dollop, and then coming back for more if necessary. It was a community tub—we all buttered our toast from its contents.

But on that day Kristen let me know how embarrassed she was when her friends came over and ate breakfast and saw all those (and I quote) "gross crumbs from somebody else's toast."

"Can't we please have a separate container of butter that no one uses for toast?" she begged. Well of course we could. And now, even six years past, on any day you can find a minimum of three tubs of I Can't Believe waiting patiently for nonguilty toast use.

And then there was the unfortunate incident involving me and Ricky Neal's favorite bird, Tweety. The turquoise-hued parakeet entered our lives on Ricky's seventh birthday and happily lived his life in the confines of a spacious red birdcage—complete with beak sharpener, mirror, climbing ladder, and water on demand.

This bird had it made.

And he loved (yes, loved) Ricky. Each morning Tweety would chirp his name over and over again, and once Ricky removed him from his cage, he would do a little parakeet happy dance—hopping back and forth from his shoulder to head with an occasional nibble to the earlobe thrown in for good measure.

Now, I'm all for my children having pets, though I wouldn't consider myself a pet lover per se. My main concern regarding creatures with fur or feathers is one of cleanliness. So over the years I found myself reminding Ricky repeatedly that Tweety might enjoy his domicile a bit more without the two-foot mound of bird droppings in the center of the cage.

And thus the years played out—until the mild spring morning I walked out on our front porch and caught a noxious whiff of Tweety's cage.

Ugh! How on earth was that bird able to breathe in that atmosphere, I wondered? But I refused to clean the cage myself. After all, he was Ricky's bird and Ricky's responsibility.

So I gently removed the cage from its hook and tenderly spoke, "Come on, Tweety, I'll take care of you. I'm going to set you outside where you can take a deep parakeet breath of fresh air."

Opening the porch screen door, I placed bird and cage on the top step and said, "Enjoy this beautiful spring day, and I'll get your useless landlord to clean your cage out tonight."

Ahhh…I just love doing kind, motherly things like that, don't you?

Five hours later a shriek pierced the house as I heard Ricky yell, "Who put my bird outside with his cage door open?!"

Gulp. (I thought about blaming Patrick.)

Yes, indeed, nothing serves up the mothering guilt quite like a beloved missing parakeet…especially when you spot a barn owl right outside your front porch window the same day. And when you factor in my track record of being a less than zealous pet lover? Well, Ricky still isn't completely convinced that was a mistake on my part.

Crumbs in the butter. Parakeets missing. Who knew motherhood could serve up such a feast of inane (or not so inane) guilty moments?

And that's what brings us to Mt. Woulda…the place where we can examine all the things we woulda done if we knew then what we know now.

This particular mountain will actually provide a rest stop on our Guiltmore trek, a place where we can relax, share a snack, and take in a little hindsight knowledge that mothers have gleaned over the ages.

I certainly woulda done scads of things differently to save myself more than a little bit of grief and guilt as a mom. And the funny thing is the vast majority of them aren't all that profound—profound as in take-your-breath-away revelation, that is.

No, most of my excursions into Guiltmore's terrain have come as the result of events, decisions, circumstances, and choices, that looking back, were altogether common to motherhood. So in the remaining pages of this chapter you will find tons of woulda comments from mothers all across this country.

I invite you to read and consider them all. And see if you can't save yourself a little worry, a little fear, and a whole lot of guilt by taking to heart what each one says.

Given the Opportunity, Moms Would Tell Other Moms…

- "Sleep whenever your teenager sleeps! I think you're up just as much, if not more, with a 17-year-old as you were when he or she was a baby. Except now you're waiting up for your teen to arrive safely home rather than trying to get out of the nursery without waking your infant up."

- "Your life isn't always in an uproar as a mother—despite what other neurotic moms may tell you."

- "Sick kids almost never go to their father's side of the bed in the middle of night to announce they feel like they're gonna barf. No, you can pretty much count on it being your side each and every time."

- "Be careful what music videos and CDs you let your kids listen to—you'll be singing the theme from *Blue's Clues* waaaay longer than they will!"

- "Grandmothers, aunts, and cousins can make wonderful baby-sitters...trust them!"

- "At the same time...trust your mothering instincts about who you leave your children with."

- "Stretch marks, saggy breasts, and bags under the eyes—and your husband [and you] will *still* be in the mood!"

- "There's no such thing as balance. It's all about choices—choosing this to gain that, giving up that to make this a reality. Choices. Not always a balanced life, but a peaceful one I think."

- "You'll get over regretting you had children. And yes, I think many moms at some point regret the losses motherhood sometimes brings, especially if they're shallow losses like 'time to put on makeup' or 'get to sleep in late on Saturdays.' But as I said, you'll get over it and will, in all probability, come to view your feelings of regret as momentary lapses of judgment. By then, of course, you'll actually be getting around to getting your makeup on and catching a few more hours of sleep."

What I've Done Right

Taking each of my children out on a date once a month. They love it, and it's the best time to catch up on what's going on in their life.

—Patti, age 48

- "Some of us are absolute control freaks. We just don't know it until that first baby arrives."

- "Write down *everything* about what happens in your family! You'll forget nearly *everything* by the time your oldest child is 15 years old. I never knew how entertaining and amusing it would be to recall Emily's (the 15-year-old) first attempt at feeding herself. I documented it all, and sometimes I catch her reading her baby book, curled up in the chair I used to nurse her in and smiling as she reads."

- "Don't make your two-year-old hold your hand constantly while walking in the mall. His poor little arm has to get tired being held straight up for so long. Carry him or push him around in a stroller."

- "Do your best to live day to day without taking on unnecessary worry about what may be."

- "Stop trying to make your child's life happy and simply (well, it's not really all that simple really) help the child discover who he or she is meant to be."

- "No mom has it all together. We're all dealing with loose ends when it comes to motherhood and our children. Some of us are just better at keeping up appearances, that's all."

Great advice, all of it, from moms who have struggled with all kinds of mothering guilt and lived to tell about it. But here's the best one of all, the one that woulda changed my life if I'd known it oh, so many years ago. Let's use it as a watchword as we pack away our snacks and begin the ascent to Mt. Inconsistency:

- "Your children won't remember half the stuff you're currently feeling guilty about."

8
Mt. Inconsistency

The Rule We Can't Live Up To

◎

*U*gh! Someone please pass the Dramamine; I'm feeling mighty queasy on this slope. But trust me—it has nothing to do with the mountainous altitude and everything to do with this oft-repeated admonition of parenting advisors and child-rearing professionals everywhere to mothers trekking across Guiltmore's terrain. It's been written in magazines, published in books, and articulated across television and radio airwaves ad nauseam and sounds a little bit like this: *Consistency is the most important element in effective parenting.*

Sigh.

How could I or any other mother possibly forget this dire warning when we've been bombarded with its guilt-inducing power since day one of parenting? For instance, think back to chapter 1, where I told you all about my plans for being a perfect mother and doing everything right while pregnant. You may recall that part of my doing things right entailed swallowing horse-sized prenatal tablets.

Now, had I actually been a horse rather than just feeling like one, I could have easily digested said tablets and slept peacefully for the next six months. But alas, I suffer with a very sensitive gag reflex disorder. I tend to throw up anything I swallow that is larger than an M&M.

Not surprisingly, no matter how many clever ways I tried to get those horse tablets down…well, they tended to come back up. Sometimes I would manage to get one down. The next day, all my efforts would be unsuccessful. And eventually, after day after day of grossing my husband out with my dramatic dry heaves at the breakfast table and chopping the vitamins into seemingly doable pieces and attempting to consume said pills in the late night hours, all to no avail, I stopped trying. Which means I was unable to *consistently* ingest the recommended vitamins and minerals that all the pregnancy experts said I needed. I spent the following weeks paralyzed with fear that my failure of consistency would do irreparable harm to my baby.

Now, some of you reading this may think I'm crazy, but I know that more than a few of you can relate to how this little story plays out. You too have felt inconsistent in some area and have beaten yourself up about it both then and over the years.

You too have read the books, listened to the experts, heeded the authorities, and acquired your own lists of things you must do consistently, only to find yourself missing the mark—and feeling very guilty and more than a little bit sick in the process. (Here, you don't look so good, take one of my *chewable* Dramamines and then continue reading my sad, inconsistent little tale.)

Okay, so here's how it happened.

My Inconsistent Adventures with Folic Acid

For the first four months of my pregnancy, I did not take those prenatal vitamins consistently. And month by month, as I read the three foot by three foot label on that monstrous jar, all I could think about was all the healthy nutrients my baby *wasn't* getting due to my inability to swallow those horse pills. I was especially worried about my inconsistent supply of folic acid.

See, in 1987 you couldn't pick up a baby magazine or tune into a child health program without someone proclaiming the miracle of taking folic acid before one even became pregnant. Yikes! I hadn't even heard of folic acid prior to my first OB visit. Now I was learning that folic acid, sometimes called foliate, is a B vitamin found mostly in leafy green vegetables like kale or spinach, as well as legumes, orange juice, and enriched grains. All you have to do is turn back to chapter 2 ("A Base-Camp Confession") and my statement about fruits and vegetables to realize that the chances of my having consumed sufficient foliate through my diet were slim to none.

So naturally I felt guilty.

Then I read another book that gave detailed accounts of repeated medical studies showing that women who got a certain number of milligrams daily prior to and during conception dramatically reduced—by up to 70 percent!—the risk of their baby being born with a serious neural defect.

Well, that was just dandy. Here I was, a non-kale-consuming pregnant woman who only ate spinach in a cheese and artichoke dip, and I couldn't swallow those all-important vitamins either. I did my best with orange juice and "enriched" bread, but in my heart I knew that wasn't enough.

I thought my baby was doomed! Even so, I was looking forward to my first sonogram. Then, at last, I would know the verdict.

A few weeks passed, and at last I found myself lying flat on my back, bladder heavily distended, as a technician spurted ice-cold gel on my abdomen and methodically moved an equally cold paddle across its expanse. This was in the old days, mind you, before sonograms showed near-photographic images of the tiny babe nestled safely within your womb. Back then, they were a mite blurry—almost indistinguishable to the unpracticed eye.

"Oh, look, Rick, you can see the baby's leg," I exclaimed. "Hm…

actually, that's just a scratch on the screen, ma'am," the sonographer replied.

Once we had that sorted out, though, we were good to go, and I could hardly believe what my eyes beheld. There before my eyes was my daughter—all 14, non-folic-acid weeks' worth of her.

And she was beautiful.

I gazed at her arms—two of them, with fingers attached.

I gazed at her legs—two of these also, with ten toes presumably there (the fuzz factor played in at this point a bit).

I watched her tiny heart beat and heard mine, stronger and dominant, accompanying the sweet refrain.

I gazed at her spinal cord (intact and healthy) and then caught a glance of something else entirely.

Gulp!

As the sonographer cluelessly chatted away with my husband and moved the paddle away from what I had just seen, my hands became clammy, and my heart rate on the screen jumped noticeably.

"Quick!" I urged her. "Put the paddle back to where you just had it. I think there's something wrong!"

Bless that dear woman's heart. She didn't say a word, nor did she change her facial expression. She simply did as I had asked (demanded?) and then calmly asked, "What did you see that upset you, Julie?"

Oh, boy. She should have never asked.

With nary a thought, I dove into my folic-acid litany of fear and apprehension. I apologized profusely for every green M&M I had ever eaten, every green vegetable I had failed to consume. I verbally chastised myself for my inability to perform the most elementary exercise in motherhood—swallowing pills that were good for my baby. And then I told her what I thought I had seen a few seconds before.

I was convinced my baby had no neck!

Bless that dear woman's heart again. She didn't laugh. She didn't roll her eyes. She didn't tell me I was an utter goofball. No, she simply looked me full in the face and smiled gently. "Here, let me show you how shadows can make you see things that aren't really there." And she did. For four or five minutes she took the time to freeze the image and pointed out bony landmarks that clearly indicated my daughter did indeed possess everything she needed to eventually hold her head up.

Moment by moment, the apprehension of believing I may have done irreparable harm to my baby was relieved. Second by second, the first of many anxious, guilt-ridden excursions up Mt. Inconsistency was completed. And I learned that it's possible to be just a little bit too paranoid about consistency.

What I've Done Right

Forgiving my children's father when he committed adultery. My kids know what it means to have a family restored by the grace and power of God.

—Irene, age 56

Rethinking Consistency

Before I go any further, let's get one thing straight: I still think consistency is important. Children need consistent parenting in order to feel secure. And it goes without saying—though I'll say it anyway—that we moms do sometimes confuse our children with inconsistent, contradictory directives or behavior. Such contradictions can indeed be detrimental to both us and our children.

For instance, telling your young child one day that she cannot cross a busy intersection by herself, allowing her to do so the next, and then enforcing the rule on another day is confusing at best—life threatening at worst. And here's another example, pulled straight from the parenting memories of yours truly. Preventing your first two children from watching PG-13 movies until they are 13 but then allowing your third-born to do so because you're simply too tired to deal with the issue is not an example of first-rate parenting. And yes, I've carried plenty of guilt around about this one. Patrick seemed to have a much shorter period of childhood innocence thanks to my loosening the reins of consistency, and a part of me has grieved over that as his mom. I've also had to cope with understandable resentment from my older two; they're right to think my inconsistency was unfair.

And I, like many other moms, have come to regret the inconsistency traps I've sometimes laid for myself and my children. Those are the rules or punishments I've decreed but had no real intention of enforcing. (Many would be impossible to enforce.) Come on, I know a few of you drama divas like me have done this too—shrilly threatened lifetime groundings and otherwise unrealistic threats and punishments. Such threats are just empty words we use to get our own way or to control our children. The trouble is, they invite our children to distrust us and ignore our warnings.

Children thrive on predictability, on repetition. In order to grow into healthy, balanced adults, they need to know what to expect from us. They need to be able to count on both our affection and our discipline, and they need to be able to trust our promises. Creating a home environment that generates peaceful assurance and reasonable expectations for mother and child alike is absolutely worth the effort.

Consistency, in other words, is a worthwhile goal.

But if your goal is absolute consistency, I'd suggest you reconsider—because absolute consistency in *anything* is not possible for actual human beings.

Think about it. What is absolute consistency but perfection? And what human being is perfect? You *know* the answer to that one. (We've already established that Mt. Immaculate Perfection is a mirage.)

So I believe we can reduce a lot of our guilt over inconsistency by revising our conception of what consistent parenting really means. Now be honest. What do you think of when you picture consistency? Probably what I've always thought of:

No error.

No deviating from the projected goal.

No mistakes.

No room for a little thing called being human.

And like I said…impossible.

But if you actually take a minute to look up the word, you'll see that consistency is not at all the same thing as perfection. My dictionary defines consistency as "showing steady conformity to character, profession, belief, or custom."

Aha! Did you catch that? Did you note two small but key words: *steady* and *conformity?*

Steady *adj.* : direct or sure in movement

Conformity *n* : action in accordance with some specified standard or authority

Steady conformity *n* : the direct or sure movement or action in accordance with some specified standard or authority

Well, that's different, isn't it? Consistency in my life as a mother, be it in the arena of discipline, education, setting house rules and guidelines, or resolving conflict, isn't the all-or-nothing kind of thing I thought it was. It doesn't mean absolute, unwavering perfection. It's more a matter of forward motion in the right direction over the long haul. That's the kind of consistency we mothers can realistically aim for.

Does that mean we'll will never go off course? Afraid not.

But it does mean that when we do catch ourselves veering left or right, we can then steer back in the right direction. It's the overall course that counts—and that's true whether we're dealing with babies who won't go to sleep without being held, toddlers who want to hijack the bed, or teenagers who know we'll probably be sleeping on the living room couch when they get in just before curfew.

Our children really don't need us to be perfect or unwavering. But we'll all do best—and feel a lot less guilty—when we aim for steady, principled, and yes, consistent parenting.

A Matter of Principle

Of course, it's hard to be steady and principled without a fairly clear understanding of what your principles are.

Which leads me to ask, are you parenting on purpose? Have you actually considered what your parenting ideas, beliefs, and objectives are?

I'm talking about actually verbalizing your principles, looking them in the face, even writing them down. That's a great way to increase your chances of "steady conformity to character, profession, belief, or custom."

One of the most helpful ways I've found to pinpoint my parenting principles is to ask myself two simple questions about any issue that comes up:

1. In the light of eternity, does this really matter?

2. In the light of eternity, what does matter?

It's amazing how simply thinking through the answers to those questions (let alone writing them down or verbalizing them) can help you get a grip on what's truly worth your time, effort, and attention. Steering a steady course is easier if you know where you want to go. So a steady conformity in your mothering ways will be a bit easier if you can confidently state the overall direction in which you are purposefully moving.

So, how about it?

Name one overarching belief you hold as a template for your decisions and actions as a mom. Or identify one of the key objectives you have in this sometimes messy, always surprising task of raising the next generation of men and women. (Deep gulp.)

Here are a couple of mine.

One of my core objectives as a mother has been teaching and demonstrating a healthy respect for people in positions of authority so that my children might naturally come to have a sincere and genuine respect for their father, me, and God. I'll grant you that's a tall order. But I've tried my best to align my actions, my deeds, my words, and my nonverbal communications with that principle. Keeping it in mind has helped me to bite my tongue when I was ready to pop off with something flippant, to show respect when I wanted like anything to not show respect, and to practice and model what I believe in any number of ways.

Another objective I've had has simply been to create a home filled with laughter and joy that will draw my adult children back when they can choose to do the exact opposite. Keeping that objective in mind has sometimes pushed me to lighten up, sometimes compelled me to work a little harder to add the little extras that make home fun. It's helped me occasionally choose a day at the park together over an afternoon of chores...and also to go to the trouble of planning a big celebration when doing nothing would be far more convenient. Or—gasp!—even play a board game or two.

Just keeping in mind what I want to accomplish and what I believe God expects of me as a mother has been the key to becoming, over the years, a much more consistent, more successful, and far less guilty parent. I still can't swallow big vitamins, though. And our mealtimes still tend to be lacking in consistent greenery, though I'm getting a little better about that too.

So what about you, my mountaineering friend? Why not take the time to think a few of these things out before continuing on with the rest of the chapter. Stick a bookmark on this page or simply dog-ear the corner as I have done with any book worth coming back to. Come back from time to time and consider why you're doing what you're doing...and where you really want to go. I think you'll find you parent more consistently as a result.

Goodness knows we can dislodge a glacier load of false guilt simply by embracing the truth of *steady conformity* rather than *seamless perfection*. (Ah! See how these peaks shadow one another? Immaculate Perfection is casting a long one right about now—and it's not even a real mountain!)

And speaking of false guilt, before we move on I want to point out a few other areas where you can dump some of your guilt about consistency.

A Mother's Prerogative

It is the right and duty of every living, breathing mother to change her mind on any given situation when presented with new information of any sort. If you're the mother of teenagers or perhaps have an unbelievably savvy four-year-old living in your home (as far as I can tell, there are quite a few of these bright tots out there)—well, you're going to get called out for inconsistency in this area...and you need to dismiss that charge without a twinge of guilt.

What I've Done Right

Giving my daughters a sense of fairness.

—Gloria, age 49

Let's say on Tuesday you tell your lovable fourteen-year-old that he can spend the night at a friend's house over the weekend. He's all pumped up about the sleepover and has his PlayStation 2, paint gun, computer games, and electric guitar all packed up and waiting. Then, on Wednesday, you're sitting on the bleachers watching your nine-year-old's football game when you overhear one of your older son's classmates talking about an upcoming party at the home where your fourteen-year-old is going to be staying. Something about parents not being home...and girls coming over...and alcohol being available.

You go home, make a few calls, and change your mind about that particular sleepover.

You will of course attempt to explain to your son why there has been a change in plans.

He will of course accuse you of ruining his life.

And you will, in all likelihood, feel a little bit guilty and a whole lot inconsistent.

But hey, girlfriend, I'm telling you as a well-seasoned climber on these particular slopes, this is guilt you need to let go. Totally and completely. We don't owe our children an explanation (though we often give one) of what we believe is in their best interest. And "but you said..." doesn't matter when we discover new facts and information. Inconsistent parenting and changing your mind responsibly are not the same thing at all.

Behold the Power of Hormones

Three weeks out of the month, I can deal with just about anything.

But watch out during those seven other days! Bombastic 11-year-olds seem to stomp on every last nerve. Ricky Neal's Phil-Collins-worthy drum solos (please tell me you remember the awesome riff in the middle of "In the Air Tonight") reverberate through my brain and leave it feeling like Jell-O. And should my daughter fail to replace my Revlon "Truest Black" mascara…oh, you don't even want to know what happens.

Now, lest you consider me a hormone harpy, truly, I am not.

But I am a realist. And I have tried to teach my children (and my husband) to be realists also. Therefore, I can tell you without too much guilt that I handle some matters a bit differently when my estrogen is spiking.

I'm not a crazy female. Nor do I use my hormones as an excuse for bad behavior. (Not that I haven't tried, mind you.)

I'm simply a woman who is more prone to snappy, irritated responses when her bloated body resembles the state of Delaware. And the truth is that my track record is anything but consistent during these times. I often wake up half mad, and chances are slim to none that I'll allow any overnight stays of walking, talking, giggling, burping, belching…even breathing!…best friends. (This is, of course, in direct opposition to my manner of thought and action during the other three weeks, when I am almost always sweet, reasonable, and tolerant. And don't let my children read this!) After all, it wouldn't do to have children running back home spreading rumors about the bloated Barnhill mom.

I tend to get emotional during this week too. So it isn't uncommon for me to tear up at the dinner table as I take in the Waltonesque qualities of my little family. You remember *The Waltons,* don't you? It was a 1970s-era TV show about a strong, loving family during the Great Depression. And if you don't remember it, just use your imagination and think *heartwarming.* There's Pa, sitting at the head of the table, threatening to ground Jim Bob for the rest of his natural life if he dares poot at the table again. And there's dear older sister Mary Ellen sweetly requesting that her youngest brother Ben be told to breathe away from her side of the table...

Well, maybe *The Barnhills* doesn't quite warm anyone's heart but mine...

At any rate, my kids have learned to go with the ups and downs of Hormone Week, and I have done my best to encourage them to be empathetic. I tell my boys they will someday have wives who will love them beyond measure due to their ability to not only spot a hormone shift from 30 paces but to honor all that such a shift might entail.

And for my daughter—well, I like to believe she will one day grow up and call me blessed. But not bloated.

And since my monthly...um, changes come on a fairly predictable schedule, I choose to think of them as both steady and conformed to normal human female biology.

Nothing inconsistent there, right?

9
Mt. Unimaginable

When Your Worst Fears Come True

◎

An acquaintance of mine gave birth to a healthy baby boy about six years ago. He was her firstborn, and she and her husband doted on him like crazy. Like many first-time mothers, she seriously contemplated the risks and benefits of subjecting her baby to the mandatory child vaccine regulations imposed by her state.

She did what I did—she read every article, book, and medical journal report she could get her hands on, contemplated the pros and cons of each choice, read through the preposterous medical disclaimers regarding each immunization, and eventually came to the conclusion that she would allow her baby to be vaccinated.

And so it began. Her son's first shots were administered within weeks of his birth, and all appeared to go well. Over the course of nearly 20 months, she willingly subjected her growing toddler to these disease-controlling injections.

But somewhere along the way, my friend's young son began to change. The changes at first were imperceptible to anyone other than a mother. But gradually she observed a marked difference in his temperament as well as increased emotional withdrawal from other family members and—more worrisome still—from herself.

She didn't dismiss her worries or unsettling observations. Instead, she made appointment after appointment with her family pediatrician until he referred her to a specialist who he believed might be able to allay her worries.

He didn't.

Instead, upon close observation and after a thorough check of her son's medical background and developmental behavior, the specialist confirmed rather than alleviated my friend's greatest fears. He told her the boy was now suffering from a subtle form of autism—a disorder that a growing number of medical authorities within the health care community believe can be brought about by the very vaccines my friend had allowed.

Unimaginable.

Did the vaccines contribute to that little boy's autism? I honestly don't know. And I'm certainly not suggesting that you not vaccinate your own children. An honest disagreement on this issue exists among the medical community as well as between educated parents. And the outcome could have been just as unimaginable had my friend *not* vaccinated and her child had succumbed to one of the diseases the shots would have protected him against.

My intent is not to stir up fear or make anyone out to be the bad guy. In fact, this particular story has no bad guy or good guy. However, now a young mother can't seem to find her way off one of Guiltmore's most brutal slopes. Whether you agree or disagree with my friend's conclusion that she shouldn't have vaccinated her son, she is still a mother just like you and me whose heart and dreams have been crumpled like a paper cup by her journey up Mt. Unimaginable.

The Chapter I Didn't Want to Write

Every book I've written has included one particular chapter that was nearly impossible to write. Each time I procrastinate, wary of putting words on the page that may come across as blasé, trite, or preachy regarding important and weighty matters. Or perhaps I just don't want to think about the painful truth the chapter needs to address or the possible fallout of addressing it.

In my first book, *She's Gonna Blow!*, chapter 5 kept me staring blankly at a computer monitor. That was the chapter called "Volcanic Damage: Recognizing When You've Gone Too Far." It needed to be written, demanded to be told, but I wasn't so convinced the world (particularly the Christian publishing world) was going to like what I had to say. And to tell the truth, I wasn't all that happy about saying it—especially since it applied directly to me.

Chapter 15 of *'Til Debt Do Us Part* was the next. That chapter opened with the words, "I never thought I'd leave my marriage..." And believe me, typing those lines wasn't exactly the easiest thing for me to do.

With *Scandalous Grace* the problem chapter was titled "Scorched Places"; it had me peeling back the veneer of a life spent pretending everything was okay when in fact it was falling apart at the seams. Ouch. Chapter 9 of *Radical Forgiveness* kept me sending fitful e-mails to my editor and muttering out loud to no one in particular, "This is definitely my last book!" And I believed it—until chapter 4 ("How Are You, Really?") in *Exquisite Hope* needed to be written.[5]

Well, today I add "Mt. Unimaginable" to my list of chapters I didn't want to write. Read on. I believe you'll understand why.

In this particular chapter I find myself more observer than participant, a writing conduit for those who have experienced the life-shattering loss of a child or sat helplessly by as their dreams and hopes for their children's lives were ripped away. And for those, especially, who believe that they were somehow responsible for what happened.

I cannot begin to understand what such grief and guilt feels like. To be honest, I don't *want* to understand it—because only those who have experienced it can truly know what it feels like. Just hearing the stories I share in this chapter is difficult enough.

And yet I am confident of this one thing: If a mother has any hope of surviving this treacherous peak and reaching a vista of grace, that hope will come solely through God's promised abiding presence in the face of cataclysmic loss. And the healing power of grace and mercy poured out in the stories we share will be the protective barrier against that punishing avalanche of pain that accompanies a hike up Mt. Unimaginable.

What I've Done Right

Answering my children's questions honestly.

—Mia, age 33

One Mother's Story

The following e-mail came to me after an event where I had spoken on motherhood and guilt. I have permission from its author to print it here, though all names and some minor details have been changed in an effort to protect the lives of those involved.

> I don't know if you will actually receive this e-mail or not. I know some authors and speakers have their messages directed to an assistant or something. And I don't know if you'll even want to respond to me should you actually read this. It's happened before, and it certainly wouldn't surprise me.
>
> This weekend you spoke on the subject of motherhood and guilt. My ears perked up when I heard you express your desire to allow all mothers an opportunity

to tell their own stories and to reassure them that they weren't the only ones who believed they were the absolutely worst moms on the face of the planet.

I can't say I've ever heard a speaker say those words. Or allow for that fact that some of us have horrific secrets and carry even more horrific memories of making the wrong choice or decision and then having to live under its guilt.

I hope you meant what you said. Not many people know my story, and I find it hard to believe that other mothers live with the garbage I live with each and every day of my life. I do feel all alone—would you please tell me if I'm not?

Four years ago, I was the mother of two children—my oldest, a four-year-old girl, and her baby brother, just 20 months younger. I remember you saying your two oldest were 18 months apart, and I almost wanted to vomit in my seat.

You see, anything and everything reminds me of my loss. Of my mistake (and that isn't even close to the right word). Of my guilt. Four years ago, I decided to take the children to our local park in hopes of wearing them out before nap time. I felt totally overwhelmed as a mom, and more days than not I wished I could just have a few quiet hours to myself without having to feed, change, burp, rock, or chase after someone.

That's exactly what I thought on my way to the park. I had strapped both children into their car seats and was driving along when I heard my daughter unsnap her seat and then felt her begin to climb over into the front seat. She had done this numerous times before, and I was totally fed up with it. I turned my head back toward her and screamed, "Get back in your car seat right now!"

I know I must have looked awful at that moment— yelling, screaming, and threatening.

She was scurrying back to her seat while I continued shouting, "I refuse to pull over and buckle you up this time, Sarah! Mommy is so tired of you disobeying her."

And those were the last words she'd ever hear me speak.

Seconds later, an approaching car veered off the shoulder, overcompensated with steering, lost complete control, and crashed head-on into me and my children.

Witnesses say our car crumpled like an accordion. And in less time than it took me to speak those final words, my daughter's life ended. My son and I survived—both protected by a safety belt or seat.

It's been four years since that awful day, and there hasn't been a day or even a minute that I haven't thought of her and asked myself why I didn't simply pull over and deal with my incredibly independent, beautiful, talkative, and living, breathing daughter.

No amount of jail time or fines compares to the penalty of guilt I deal with for allowing something so awful to happen to my baby. Nothing—absolutely nothing. I'm desperate to believe there is hope for me. I hope I can find that peace and rest that you spoke about in your own life and in the lives of other moms. I hope you will believe me when I tell you I love my daughter with all my heart. And I hope you will tell my story—

be it in a book or from a platform—because perhaps there is another mom out there who feels she is the only one living with the awful consequences of her action or inaction. Perhaps there is someone else living with the unimaginable.

Can you see why I hesitate to write chapters like this? And yet this is why they must be written.

I recognize it could have been me writing a similar e-mail. You see, in 1990, I threw my not-quite-two-year-old daughter onto her bed in a fit of uncontrolled rage and watched as her tiny frame made contact against a cold, hard bedroom wall. Even now, after 16 years and multiple reassurances from Kristen, thinking about that day still feels like a punch to the gut. I'm painfully aware that if any number of varying factors had worked differently, I could have been the one mourning and shaking with grief. I'm not exaggerating.

What I've Done Right

I never gave up as a mom. I've wanted to at times, but I kept on keeping on, and I think my children will come to value that as they become adults.

—Helen, age 36

About two weeks after my abusive act towards Kristen, in fact, I read in a national newspaper of a mother who did nearly the exact same thing I did. Except this woman's child somehow hit a metal curtain rod, which pierced her right temple and killed her.

I nearly threw up after reading that article years ago. And have thought about that mother time after time ever since, for I fit the description I read of her to an absolute T. She too was a middle-class, stay-at-home mother with no prior history of such actions. She too was a woman no one would ever expect to act out in such a manner. I don't know if she was charged with murder or some equally horrific crime.

I don't know if she had other children.

I don't know how she's held up beneath the guilt and shame of the unimaginable.

And I don't know if anyone has ever told her there is hope, forgiveness, and grace even for the unimaginable, but I keep on praying for her and holding out hope for her as well as for me and you.

Healing for Unimaginable Guilt?

So what do we mothers do when the unimaginable happens?

Most likely, we blame ourselves. We may fixate on choices we made, fatal mistakes, or moments of rage that resulted in the unthinkable. And even if we did nothing to cause the tragedy, we may berate ourselves for not controlling, for not foreseeing, for not doing or being or believing some way or some thing that could have prevented it all from occurring.

My friend with the autistic son still hasn't let go of the guilt she carries after allowing her son to receive those shots. We have spoken time and time again, and the basic flow of our conversation seldom varies.

I tell her it's not her fault.

She tells me she should have researched harder and asked more questions.

I tell her she could not possibly have known what would happen.

She tells me that if she had trusted her first instinct, it wouldn't have happened.

I tell her she needs to forgive herself and let go of her guilt.

She tells me she would have done so years ago if she believed it were possible.

And there, of course, but for the grace of God, go I. And you too, perhaps—unless you're one of those moms who have found their way to Mt. Unimaginable without a sherpa.

The terrifying truth is that it could happen to any of us. Any one of us, regardless of how passionately she loves her children, is capable of turning her back for a minute, forgetfully locking a child in a car, or striking out in anger. The issues of guilt are really the same, but the pain level is amped up so high that merely surviving requires extra grace.

But a comforting truth is available even on this bleak and craggy summit.

The grace of God reaches out to that mother. And to you too if you are one of those who have already found yourself on the slopes of Mt. Unimaginable. For though the pain is deeper and the road to healing is steeper than for other forms of guilt, the solution is essentially the same.

I hesitate even to say this because I don't want to minimize your pain or mock your grief. But it's true. The rocky trail down from Mt. Imaginable winds in the same direction as the trail from all the other peaks, and it follows the same downhill (if sometimes rocky and winding or almost impassable) path.

The path down from Mt. Imaginable is the trail you're already on—the trail of God's unimaginable grace.

Read on...

10

The Downhill Trek

Sherpa Mom's Practical Guide to Getting Out of Guiltmore

The air has grown decidedly thinner as we've negotiated the higher passes in Guiltmore National Park. The path we follow has become conspicuously narrow and requires everyone's utmost attention. Where sometimes before we were able to casually amble alongside one another as we explored a particular slope, here icy blasts of doubt and fear force us to move forward in solitary formation.

But don't forget, you are not alone.

Give that rope a tug and remind yourself of the women who are just ahead as well as those following behind. At times during this journey, you may feel you're out here all by yourself. You may even wonder if Sherpa Mom has cut out and chosen to leave you flapping in the wind alone.

But I haven't. Nor, for that matter, has God. And that's the most important thing to keep in mind as you leave behind the summit of Unimaginable and begin to negotiate the downhill slopes of Guiltmore.

That's right. Downhill.

Here on the back side of Mt. Imaginable, far above the tree line, we've already begun our descent toward Graceland. But though the journey really is downhill from here, we've still got some hiking to do.

Every mountain climber knows that climbing down can be as challenging as climbing up. So let's take a break before we go much farther and take a look at where we've been…and where we're going.

A Backward—and Forward—Look

By now, I hope you've done one or more of the following:

- Thought about and documented a few of the many things you've done right as a mom. (If not, go back to page 9 and do so immediately.)

- Considered a few of my guilty confessions and found a mom who is even more neurotic (or *way* more neurotic) than yourself.

- Explored and thoughtfully considered some of the formidable peaks of maternal guilt.

I also hope you are determined to deal with your own guilt and begin moving far, far, far, away from it. You're ready to get down out of this mountain range. And so am I.

In order to accomplish this, I'm going to ask you to lean into the incomparable sagelike wisdom of Yogi Berra, who once advised, "If you come to a fork in the road, take it."

Indeed!

The question, of course, is this: Which fork will take us where we need to go?

Remember, I stated in the opening chapter that I do not believe we ever vanquish guilt utterly and completely from our lives as mothers. Guiltmore National Park will always be there in our backyards, and from time to time we'll find ourselves back up on its rocky slopes.

However (and this is a big however!), we can get down from Guilt-more more quickly and keep it in the background more successfully if we can learn to deal with our guilt feelings in a healthy and effective way.

Which means learning to choose the right trail off the mountain. And just as important, knowing how to find that trail again should we find ourselves back up in the hills.

And that's what I as Sherpa Mom want for you. More than anything—more than making you laugh, more than letting you know you're not alone, and more than hearing back from you in an e-mail or a face-to-face meeting—I want to give you practical, take-away help you can implement in your very real, day-to-day life as a mom.

So catch your breath as we pause here at the crossroads and talk about choosing the best path down the slope toward Graceland. We're also going to go back and review our geography lesson. (Remember my base-camp lecture?)

Because at this juncture, the road you need to take depends entirely on the kind of guilt you're dealing with.

Why the Right Trail Matters

Here are a couple of things to keep in mind for choosing the best trail. First, there is an effective remedy for guilt—a tried-and-true way to resolve and move past it. Second, that remedy won't work on anything other than *true* guilt.

This makes sense if you think about it. And that's why we spent all that time distinguishing true guilt from false guilt. It's not just idle talk about geology. It's vital navigational knowledge. Simply put, if you're dealing with true guilt, you need to take one path. If your guilt is false, you should take another.

Let me remind you that false guilt is made up of all those vague, cloudy, "I'm not exactly sure how I messed up but I know I feel like

I did something wrong or didn't do something right" feelings that gnaw away at our confidence and chip away our faith in our mothering instincts and decisions.

False guilt is just that—false.

It is an error in truth—the guilt you feel when you haven't really done anything wrong. And *because* your guilt feelings aren't based on any kind of actual wrongdoing, nothing you do to address your guilt and find a remedy will work.

Instead, this is a guilt you just need to say no to. Later, we will consider the difficult but necessary path of dealing with your true guilt. But right now you can choose to simply leave your false guilt behind.

Do you find it difficult to tell the difference? Asking yourself the following questions might help:

• Did I really do something wrong? (Just being in the wrong place at the wrong time doesn't count.)

• Under the circumstances (given what I knew and who I was), could I really have acted differently?

• Who says I shoulda-coulda-woulda done otherwise? (Just because your mother said you should—or your neighbor or even your pastor—that doesn't necessarily mean you shoulda-coulda-woulda. That's really a matter for God and your own conscience.)

• Am I confusing feelings of *shame* ("I'm unworthy as a person), *grief* ("I'm very sad or depressed that this happened"), *fear* ("What if this causes something awful to happen?"), *embarrassment* ("I can't believe I let that happen!"), or just *uneasy feelings* with an actual state of guilt?

- Is this a *control* issue—am I assuming responsibility for something that I really can't control and have no business trying?
- Is this issue actually worth worrying about? (Sometimes even true guilt can be so trivial and unimportant in the big scheme of things that it's practically the same as false guilt.)

As you explore those questions and answer them honestly, you should begin to get a sense of what's really going on with your guilt feelings and how you need to handle them.

Here's an example. Maybe your guilt has something to do with the way your children behaved in public—um, maybe just an hour or two ago! And yes, this is another example from my own personal guilt files. But every mother on the face of the earth knows what it's like to have their kid do or say something utterly and completely stupid in public.

My children in particular have always chosen to ask the following question within earshot of a man or woman I have just engaged in conversation, "Mom, what's his (or her) name?" They do this time after time despite my repeated warnings. And time after time, I am rendered speechless and embarrassed and, yes, guilty because 1) my brain has no clue whom I just spent 12 minutes chattering away with, and 2) I think I really should have managed to teach my children better manners.

But you know what?

I have decided not to feel guilty about this any longer. Because try as I may, I simply can't control if and when my children will ask me that question. And try as I may, I simply cannot control the level of memory recovery my brain does or does not provide in those moments of interrogation.

Here's another false guilt you may be able to relate to.

Maybe you've found yourself in the position of needing to place your child in daycare. And despite the fact that you've researched the facility, checked out the caregiver, and felt confident your child would be tended to by a loving and kind adult, you still battle that vague, cloudy feeling of having done something bad or wrong.

I remember when Kristen and Ricky Neal were just six and four years old and I found myself needing to substitute teach as much as possible to keep things going financially. I was able to send Kristen to kindergarten, but I had to find somewhere for Ricky Neal to stay. I checked out a couple of daycare facilities and finally settled on one.

He lasted all of two days.

And I felt guilty about those two days for close to ten years, until one day I looked at him and realized he had somehow managed to thrive despite those 16 hours of confinement at Robin Redbreast Daycare. What's more, I had done the best I could at the time. And when trouble arose, I had responded quickly. In this particular instance, I really wasn't guilty. So the only reasonable thing I could do with my guilty feelings was tell them no and leave them behind.

What I've Done Right

Letting the children see me pray and read the Bible. I think you lead by example more than words.

—Shelly, age 68

False guilt can have us walking down all sorts of dead-end trails. Maybe you're a mom who has beaten herself up for delivering a baby via C-section. Perhaps, despite your best efforts, you were unable to nurse successfully. Or your work schedule limited your ability to volunteer at your son's school. Or you're hopeless in math and have never been able to help your daughter with algebra. Or you discover in retrospect that your child's dangerous allergy to peanuts *might* have been triggered by all that peanut butter you consumed during pregnancy. Or your teenager has experimented with drugs, and you can't help but wonder if you're somehow at fault.

Now, any of these situations—or a hundred more—might include an *element* of true guilt. Perhaps you really were lax in your prenatal care or making excuses about your work. Perhaps you did contribute to your child's allergies or addictions. If so, the trail I will describe in the next section will take you where you need to go. But if you've been wandering the twisted paths of false guilt, now is the time to choose another trail—one comprised of truth rather than error. Speaking truth, believing truth, and acknowledging truth will help keep your feet from slipping—and steadily move you downhill.

So what trail should you take to get rid of false guilt?

Here's a surprise: You might not need to take any trail at all. Acknowledging your feelings for what they are might be enough. You can simply look honestly at what you've been doing, realize you're not really guilty, and tell yourself it's time to stop worrying about it.

Sometimes (thank God!) it really is that easy. You just click your ruby slippers together, whisper "I'm really not guilty," and presto—you're home!

Sometimes, in the case of true-but-trivial guilt, a quick apology and a correction of course is all you really need. So you let your child have a cookie before dinner because you were too tired or distracted to say no. So you snapped at your husband when he asked you a perfectly reasonable question. If it's a single lapse and not part of a nutritional neglect pattern or chronic bad temper, your best and wisest course may be simply to say "I'm sorry" if appropriate, correct your course, and focus your energy on more important matters.

But at times you might find your false guilt harder to release, especially if you've lived with it for a long time or if it's gotten mixed up with other feelings.

You might need to argue with the voices that tell you that you should or shouldn't live a certain way. You might need to seek out paths for handling your shame or grief or your fear or your control issues. (See chapter 11 for some more about control.) You certainly need to pray for God's help to heal your pain or change faulty patterns of thinking. And if your sense of guilt persists, you may even want to consider that something deeper is going on and seek some sort of counseling.

But even in those cases, recognizing that your guilt is false is a giant step down the (right) trail to Graceland.

The Trail Down from (True) Guiltmore

I'd love to tell you that all the guilt I've felt over the years as a mom was either false guilt or a matter of taking on something that simply didn't matter in the grand scheme of life. But you've already read enough to know better.

There have been and there will be instances when entering a guilty plea is the only honest thing left to do.

Yes, it was me. I did it. It really was my fault.

In those cases, guilt feelings are valuable landmarks—absolutely appropriate signs that I need to make some changes and do a little hiking. Those steps are not necessarily fun, but they are absolutely crucial. (Guiltmore is there in the backyard for a reason.)

The good news is this: A true, dependable remedy for coping with our true guilt is available. Sherpa Mom knows the way down the mountain—though she doesn't always take it as quickly as she should.

This trail down involves a classic process outlined in the Bible and recommended by lots of authors and self-help programs. It's so basic I almost hesitate to point it out to you. But it doesn't always look that obvious when you're lost on Guiltmore and trying to find your way through the underbrush. Besides, it works. It's truly made all the difference in my own walk toward living in grace and enjoying motherhood. So I'll just lead you down the trail and trust the journey will be helpful for you.

What trail am I talking about?

It's the time-honored process of...

- acknowledging your guilt,
- confessing your guilt,
- asking forgiveness (and accepting it), and
- making amends and working toward restoration.

Maybe I can illustrate this process best by showing how it worked in my own journey away from guilt. Looking back in my journal, I find an entry dated August 28, 1994. These sobering words mark the first trailhead in my journey down, the moment when I first admitted my guilt:

> There's no other way to say it...I am guilty of being an angry, hateful, irrational mother. I have hurt the kids with my words. I have hurt them physically when I am out of control. I am guilty...

However, I didn't stop there. I had realized by this point that *feeling* bad or shameful about my behavior simply wasn't going to be enough to change me. It certainly wouldn't stop the cycle of uncontrolled anger. If anything, those guilt feelings simply set me more on edge and made me *more* likely to lash out toward my children.

So I took another step—a step of faith in many ways. I not only admitted my guilt to myself but also confessed it to God. I told all the ugly, burdensome, and shame-ridden realities of my life to the Guide who was just waiting to hear my cry for help:

> I am guilty, and I want to confess as honestly and openly as I possibly can to You, God. You have watched me as I go about my life as a mother. You know everything, good and bad, that I have said and thought and done and acted upon. And right now, today, I confess that I am guilty of mistreating my children. I ask for forgiveness from You as well as the ability to forgive myself for all the things I regret and now feel so ashamed about.

Talk about painful! I poured out on paper the ugly, guilty reality of what I had done. But I also took the next step. I asked God for forgiveness. And in that sliver of time more than 11 years ago, God did what He promises us He will always do if we will simply ask—He forgave me. And somehow, in a way only God can accomplish, He gave me the grace I needed to set aside all those ugly memories, all those shameful secrets, and all those matters of regret.

It didn't happen all at once. That's important for you to know.

And I didn't stop my hurtful behavior all at once. My habit of anger was too entrenched for that.

But gradually, over time—remember that "steady conformity" thing!—I did change. My load of guilty feelings lightened, and I began to change both my outward behavior and my inward attitude. I apologized to my children and my husband. I also worked very hard—with much prayer, a fair amount of counseling, and some antidepressant medication—to change both my unreasonable thinking and my inexcusable behavior.

Today I can honestly say that I am no longer the angry, bitter woman I once was with my children. I truly feel I have been rescued and restored. And though the change took a lot of hard work on my part, I firmly believe God changed me through the process of acknowledgment, confession, forgiveness, and restoration. In the process, He taught me what to do with my recurring guilt. I recognize the trail now. I even know it well enough to lead others.

What I've Done Right

Maintaining a positive home environment in the midst of financial hardships, divorce, and depression.

—Tanya, age 52

I believe God can and will do the same for you. After all, it's what He loves to do. He loves to take circumstances and situations that you and I may consider a lost cause and redeem them. He delights in doing the seemingly impossible—being free from angry, guilty mothering seemed beyond impossible!—and stands ready to act as the Guide for every aspect of our lives as women and as mothers.

Let me repeat this: God is the Guide. He is the Leader of this expedition. Because even as Sherpa Mom I know my place. I can show you the way as a fellow traveler. But the foundational truth of Guiltmore is that you'll never get off the mountain without the Guide!

So with that warning in mind, let's move on. Think about the "I know I'm guilty" guilt you're ready to be free from. (You may be thinking of a dozen things you're guilty of, but I suggest that you address them individually and deal with them one at a time.)

If you feel comfortable doing so, write your acknowledgment down here on the page like this:

I am guilty of _____

_____.

Or speak your admission aloud so you can hear yourself say it. The key thing is to own up to the truth of your own guilt.

The next step is to confess your guilt to God, to yourself, and perhaps to another person. Confessing to a trusted friend or counselor might be helpful as well. Admitting your guilt to another person makes it seem even more real. Or you could simply write your confession in a journal or say it as a prayer. You don't have to grovel or hang sackcloth and ashes around your shoulders and face. Simply put your guilt into words. Perhaps you'll say something similar to this:

> Right here, right now, I want to confess to You, God, as
> well as to myself that I am guilty of _____
>
> _____.

Once you've confessed, the next step is to ask forgiveness—the divine forgiveness God offers as well as the ability to forgive yourself for what you said, did, thought, or believed. Again, putting it in words is important. It can be as simple as asking this:

> God, I know I have done wrong, and right now I am
> asking for Your forgiveness. Clean my heart, my mind,
> my soul, and my memories from any and all guilt. Forgive me as only You can forgive, God, and help me let
> go of the guilt I often use against myself when thinking
> of this wrong.

Once you have confessed and asked forgiveness, it's done. It really is. The God of mercy and grace has promised just that in Scriptures such as 1 John 1:9: "If we confess our sins, He is faithful and righteous to forgive us our sins and to cleanse us from all unrighteousness" (NASB). He even says that once He has forgiven us, He completely forgets about our sins (see Jeremiah 31:34).

With that in mind, I'd like for you to purposely choose to say no to that same guilt when it beckons again. And it might! If you have confessed and asked forgiveness, you really are forgiven, but being forgiven and *feeling* forgiven can be two completely different things. You may be tempted to mull over what you've done wrong and even go through the whole process again. But what you're feeling now is false guilt—which means that God's remedy of acknowledgment, confession, forgiveness, and restoration simply don't apply anymore. He's already forgotten your guilt, remember?

So as soon as your false, residual guilt rears its ugly head, I want you to shout out the truth! Instead of meandering down a trail that has been cordoned off by forgiveness, repeat the following:

> I will not feel guilty for _____
> anymore. I have confessed my guilt. I have asked for and received forgiveness for my guilt, and I am purposefully choosing to believe the truth that it is all behind me now.

You may feel a little silly the first time you do say it—even sillier when you have to say it more than once. You may also have to ask God for grace to deal with the ongoing *consequences* of your wrongdoing because these may continue long after you have been forgiven. But trust me—the act of speaking the truth about your residual guilt will gradually shut down those lingering expressions of false guilt.

The final step I'd like you to take regarding true guilt is to do your best to make amends toward those affected by your actions and behavior.

Ugh.

I know this may sound more than a bit intimidating…or humiliating…or embarrassing…or just plain uncomfortable. If you're anything like me, you'd like to get the forgiveness and just let it go from there.

But I don't think that's an option—at least not a healthy and wise option. Our actions, behaviors, words, and deeds almost always affect someone other than ourselves. *Someone* bears the brunt of our anger, our mistakes, our willful choices, and, yes, even our sin.

It may be a child. A spouse. A parent or sibling.

It could even be someone you don't know that well—someone who just happened to be at the wrong place at the wrong time on one of those terrible, awful days when you did something that caused you guilt.

Whoever the person was, the fact remains: You've hurt someone. And that certain someone needs to hear you say "I'm sorry," to see you take ownership for the pain you have caused and do whatever is possible to right the wrong. And *you* need to do it too—the act of making amends will help you actually let go of the guilt.

You may want to speak face-to-face with the person you have hurt. In other circumstances a written letter, e-mail, or phone call might work best. If possible, back up your verbal apology with an attempt to remedy the wrong you have done. This could mean reimbursing someone financially (yes, even refilling a plundered piggybank), replacing a lost or damaged object, apologizing publicly to vindicate a person harmed by gossip…whatever it takes. Though you can't always right the wrongs you have done to others, you really do owe them an honest try. The benefit to you is that every painful act of restoration moves you yet another step down the trail to Graceland.

As you work to make amends, be sure to let the other person or persons know you are correcting your course and making specific changes that will ensure this particular wrong or hurt won't happen in the future. I've found this to be especially important in making peace with my children. I said "I'm sorry" a thousand times regarding my sarcastic mouth and tone as a mom. But when I said, "I'm sorry for being so mean with my words," and then posted on the refrigerator the actual phrase I was going to stop saying—that's when they really believed me.

Revisiting Your Memories

I don't want to imply that any of this process is easy. It sometimes is. But just as often it's a steep and rocky trail, and stumbling or getting off the path is all too easy.

In my experience, the hardest part of any trail down Guiltmore is not the actual process of acknowledging guilt, confessing, and being forgiven. What's hard is *feeling* forgiven, believing in your heart that it's taken care of, learning to leave guilt behind and live in the reality of God's grace. As I hinted earlier, this can be a problem with lingering false guilt, but it can happen in the case of real guilt as well. Guilt feelings can linger long after the actual guilt has been taken care of.

If this is true for you, I'd like to suggest that you actually reach back to those guilty places, revisit them in your memory, and recreate your emotional response to the memory so that you may begin to leave your lingering guilt behind.

Why are you looking at me like that? I'm completely serious. In fact, I have done just this (reaching back and recreating) with some of my most stubborn feelings of guilt. Writer and theology professor Lewis B. Smedes suggested the idea in his book *Forgive & Forget: Healing the Hurts We Don't Deserve.*[6] When I first read his words, I stared back at the page much as you're doing right now.

It sounded a bit…well, flaky.

But the further I read, and the more I wanted to find freedom from the "unforgivable" places of my life, the more willing I was to consider Professor Smedes' counsel.

Reluctantly at first, I pulled one guilty memory from my past and carefully appraised it with hindsight, adult maturity, biblical truth, and my all-encompassing desire for peace with my past. I considered the whys, hows, and what fors that played into its impact in my life. I reminded myself that God had taken care of my actual guilt and that I had done all I could about it. I even asked God for healing regarding this particular memory. Then I made a conscious choice about how I was going to think about what happened in the past, feel about it, and live with it in the future.

And slowly…steadily…consistently (remember those words from Mt. Inconsistency?), my response to the memory did begin to change.

I didn't hear any trumpet fanfares. I didn't see any flashes of heavenly light.

It was just as I wrote—a slow, steady, and consistent movement away from lingering guilt and discomfort toward truly accepting God's grace for that painful and guilty part of my past.

Such is the place I desire for you regarding all your guilty feelings—little and large—about being a mom. As you keep doing what we've outlined in this chapter—choosing the right trail; saying no to false guilt; walking through the process of acknowledgment, confession, forgiveness, and amends for your real guilt; and correcting your course and taking whatever steps are necessary to truly believe your freedom—you'll find yourself well on the way toward the lush green valley of Graceland.

Giving Up the Guilties
Some Quick Reminders

- When you feel overwhelmed by guilt feelings, take a deep breath and try to put things in perspective.

- Admit you can't do it all. No one can!

- Prioritize what's truly important to you. Actually write down the top five or six items. Then begin saying no (without guilt) to things that do not help you keep those priorities in line.

- When you find yourself thinking "I shoulda done (or not done)" something, ask yourself, "Who *says* I shoulda?" Who are you trying to please—your mother, your community, your friends, yourself...or God?

- When you find yourself thinking, "I coulda done (or not done) something, ask yourself, "Given the circumstances and who I was at the time, could I *really* have done that? Was it realistic or even possible?"

- When you find yourself thinking, "I woulda done that, but..." stop and consider whether you're just making excuses. Either you did or you didn't—and confronting the guilt is a lot healthier than obsessing about what might have been.

- Try turning all your shoulda-coulda-wouldas into present tense. Instead of "I shoulda done that," think "What should I or should I not do?" Instead of "I coulda," think "I can...or I can't." Instead of "I woulda," think "I will or I won't." Make your decision based on that present-tense reality.

- When you experience guilty feelings, ask yourself, "Are these feelings a symptom of true guilt, or are they the problem itself?"

- Give yourself permission to laugh at yourself. Take yourself down a peg or two (kindly), and watch the guilt diminish.

- When you feel guilty about doing or not doing something with your children, ask yourself if this issue will really matter in ten years. Fifty years? If it matters, do it. If it doesn't matter, let it go.

- Name three things you are giving your children that more money could not provide.

- Find time to rest in God. His desire is for you to experience peace, goodness, love, and rest. But you have to be still and get to know Him first.

- Ask yourself this: Is this guilty feeling a reasonable emotion? Do I honestly have something to feel guilty about? If not, let it go.

- Consider this: Am I confusing guilt with another painful emotion such as shame, grief, fear, or embarrassment?

- Know what truly makes you feel guilty—letting the groceries in the house get down to the bare bones, overscheduling both your calendar and the children's, rushing through bedtime, not spending adequate one-on-one time with each child. Do your best not to let these things sneak up on you!

- Smile more, frown less! And never underestimate the power of a good belly laugh.

- Get real about your expectations. Take a look at your expectations for yourself. Is it truly possible for you to attain all of them, all the time, without fail? Pick one or two that you'd like to strive toward and just settle into them for the next few weeks—but put the rest on indefinite hold.

- Compliment another mother. Look for opportunities to ease someone else's guilt.

- Quit gossiping about other moms and the wrong ways they do things.

- Forgive yourself. Let go of resentment or self-hatred you may hold against yourself for failing to achieve what you believe you should have as a mother.

- Change your obsessive shoulda-coulda-woulda thoughts. Yes, change! You have a choice...choose to think differently.

- Lean into the process of mothering rather than the outcome. Try to enjoy it!

- Recognize that some guilt is good for you—it can lead you to God for help and forgiveness.

- Admit when you've made a mistake and get over it already!

- Pray to know what God desires for you as a mom. Rest in that knowledge and stop looking for other people to confirm it. Practice trust.

- True guilt is specific: You know why you're feeling guilty and what you're supposed to do about it. Do it.

- Remember, God's remedy for guilt will only work if you really are guilty!

11

Almost There

Learning to (Ouch) Let Go

◎

"Are we there yet?"

Every mom knows that familiar whine. And every mom knows that if the kids are asking it, the answer is usually "Not yet, but soon."

And that is Sherpa Mom's standard response as we wind our way down Guiltmore's back slopes.

I promise you, we really are almost there. But before we get to Graceland, we've got to maneuver over some of Guiltmore's most treacherous territory. In fact, most mountain climbers will tell you the downhill trek can be even more challenging than uphill. Your calves ache. Your footing slips. You can fall. That's why on the downhill slope, especially, you must trust your Guide—and at this point I'm not talking about Sherpa Mom.

I'm talking about God, the One who made these mountains in the first place. The One who gave us guilt feelings to steer us away from wrongdoing but who also provides the remedy for our guilt and leads us to Graceland.

Truth is, if we can't trust the Guide, none of us—Sherpa Mom included—has a chance of getting off the mountain. But some of us have some problems in the trust department.

A Little Problem with Trust

Remember the question I posed about prayer way back in chapter 5? I asked myself, "Have I prayed these many prayers for and over my children because I believe God ultimately is in control…or in order that I might somehow (as impossible as it really is) control God?"

Did you notice I never actually answered that one?

That's because I've been thinking over this issue far longer than the time it took you to read the intervening pages. In fact, I've been wrestling with it since the day my daughter entered this world.

Up until an early morning hour in August 1988, I would have boldly (and honestly) told you I trusted God utterly and completely with my life and with the details of what had happened and would happen to me as an individual. I had been taught biblical truth about God's faithful and loving character from the time I was a little girl, and I had no reason to doubt this reality as I matured through my teen and college years.

I still had no reason to doubt on the day of Kristen's birth.

But I did.

I can still recall those first cloudy thoughts. They came as Kristen was sleeping in her bassinet next to my hospital bed, and I was simply watching her. Well, "simply" is an understatement if there ever was one. I couldn't take my eyes off her. I watched as she moved her head back and forth with a lovely, healthy, intact neck (the sonographer had been right!), counted the wrinkles on her pinkie finger, and laughed at her Eddie Munster hairline. I must have wrapped and unwrapped her torso a dozen times as I marveled how those same arms, legs, and feet had been kicking and moving within me a mere four hours before. My heart turned inside out and turned to maternal mush as I watched her tiny mouth form the tiniest cry.

Oh, how I loved that baby girl. And my heart would do the same number of back flips as I held and watched her brothers, Ricky Neal and Patrick. I had never known such raw, protective love until I became a mother. And I never wanted anything more in my life than I wanted to be able to keep them from any and all harm.

That's where the wrestling with God and trust comes into play. Up unto the day of my children's birth I could (and did) pray honestly, "God, whatever it takes to make me more like Jesus, that's what I want You to do. I trust You, and I know You only have my best in mind. So Your will be done…whatever."

And I'd like to tell you nothing changed after Kristen, Ricky Neal, and Patrick were born. But it did. Somewhere, somehow I found myself backing off from that childhood trust and becoming fearful of what God might or might not choose to do with me and my children.

I had no reason to fear God. I had no reason to believe God was suddenly going to act mean or vindictive toward me or my children. I had no reason not to trust.

But deep inside, I had started to believe that no one—not even God—could love those children more than I did. No one, not even God, could look out for them better than I could.

I didn't mention these feelings to a soul—not even my husband. I'm not sure I even admitted them to myself. But they were there.

The months and years passed, and I recall sitting in a study group with some other moms. One of them commented, "We need to get to a place with our faith in God where we can say, 'God, these children are not mine. They belong to You. I hold no claims on their lives. Do what You want to do with them. I take my hands off them completely.' "

Well, guess who couldn't pray that prayer?

And guess who felt guilty about that for close to 13 years?

For whatever reason—call it a lack of faith or an unhealthy desire to control—I simply could not bring myself to even come close to voicing a prayer such as that mother suggested. It seemed to me that actually praying that prayer would almost be inviting the unimaginable. But if

I *didn't* pray that prayer…well, then maybe God couldn't or wouldn't act in some negative manner against my children.

I know, it all reads crazy, and it make no theological (or mountaineering) sense. But getting to a place in my life as a mother where my trust in God superseded my maternal urge to control and yes, manipulate (in the nicest sense of the word) God's choices with my children—well, that has been the most challenging aspect of my own journey from Guiltmore to Graceland.

Trust: What's It Good For?

Is there anything more foundational to a healthy relationship than trust?

I don't believe so.

As I think back over the years I've spent with my three children, I'm reminded of the multiple times I have said to them in one way or another, "I'm your mother…trust me."

There was the icy winter morning when I had decided to drive the children to school rather than put them on the lumbering school bus that just seemed destined to land in a ditch. I made sure they were all three bundled up warmly and shouted at Ricky Neal as he barreled toward the back door, "Trust me, son—you do *not* want to go speeding down those icy back porch steps. You'll fall and hurt yourself."

Well, he was seven (and Ricky Neal), so you know what happened.

Six seconds later he was sprawled on his back nursing a rather painful headache. And while I confess a rather large part of me wanted to say, "I told you so," the other part, thankfully, just bent over, helped get him on his feet, and planted a big, fat, healing mommy kiss on his bruised head and ego.

But I still wished he had listened. He could have saved us both a lot of heartache.

More than anything, I long for my children simply to trust me.

And when I say *simply*, I mean just that. I have always wanted them to rely on my words, advice, actions, and love just as naturally and easily as they take their next breath...and the next...and the next... and the next. I've prayed they would come to have "confidence in the integrity, ability, character, and truth of a person [that would be me, their mother] or thing" (that's Webster's definition of *trust*).

See, if my children trust my integrity, my character, and my place as their mother, that very trust will afford me opportunities to speak into their lives.

I'm painfully aware that I'm fallible and human and sometimes less than trustworthy. And yet I also believe my children have been able to watch me live out my life in an authentic fashion, so perhaps I have won a place of trust in all three of their lives.

I hope so. I pray so.

Now, the connection between what I have just written and what God desires for my own life is not lost on me. Just as I long for and delight in my children's trust, God longs for me to trust Him. And God, of course, is a lot more trustworthy than I am. He knows—even when I forget—that if I could just relax and trust Him with my children and with my life in general, all of us would all be more secure, and I would struggle a lot less with issues like guilt.

What I've Done Right

I made my children go to church when they were teenagers. They didn't want to, but I insisted—no, I gave them no choice! I know I did the right thing, and they'd even tell you that if you asked them.

—Bonnie, age 51

Trusting in God rather than in my own abilities as a mother offers the ultimate source of security for my life and that of my children. In fact, the Bible encourages me (and you) to put the same kind of trust in God that we want our children to put in us. Consider these Scripture verses, which state clearly the importance of trusting God:

> The LORD's unfailing love surrounds the [mom] who trusts in him (Psalm 32:10 NIV).

> Every word of God is pure: he is a shield unto them that put their trust in him (Proverbs 30:5).

> As for God, his way is perfect; the word of the LORD is tried: he is a buckler to all them that trust in him (2 Samuel 22:31).

> In God I will praise his word, in God I have put my trust; I will not fear what flesh can do unto me (Psalm 56:4).

> Therefore we both labour and suffer reproach, because we trust in the living God, who is the Saviour of all men, specially of those that believe (1 Timothy 4:10).

But so often, especially when it comes to mothering, we insist on doing it *our* way instead of God's. When you stop and think about it, we're not so different from my seven-year-old son that icy winter morning. We barrel through life, making decisions and choices based on our own abilities and judgments rather than slowing down and listening to God's trustworthy voice and leadership. And like my son, we have nursed more than one painful headache (and heartache) as a result of not listening to God and trusting His direction.

And why do you suppose that is?

Well, I think there are as many reasons (or excuses) as there are individual mothers, but I'd like to offer a couple of suggestions. Perhaps you'll be able to identify with one or the other.

We Don't Trust God Enough

When I was a young girl, a Sunday school teacher told me something about the famous missionary Amy Carmichael that I have never forgotten. Even now, some 30 years down the road, I still recall Amy's claim that she would tuck herself into God like a small child and trust God. She said that this trust was based on a quiet and sure confidence in God's character.

Amy Carmichael believed God to be a loving, kind, and tender Father. And because she believed this, she felt confident that everything He allowed in her life was ultimately for her good.

In order to trust, in other words, you have to be convinced that the One you are trusting is actually trustworthy. And in order to be convinced, you really have to know the character of the One you're trusting.

So what do we know about God that makes Him trustworthy? Each character trait listed below is like a peg you can grasp or stand on. Or consider each one as a step on the seldom-traveled trail that crosses Guiltmore's laborious peaks and winds down the other side.

Character Peg #1: God is love (and He loves our children more than we do).

The words of 1 John 4 occupy a highlighted and note-riddled page in my beat-up New American Standard Bible, and they declare with boldness and joy the divine character of our Father:

> Beloved, let us love one another, for love is from God; and everyone who loves is born of God and knows God. The one who does not love does not know God,

for God is love. By this the love of God was manifested in us, that God has sent His only begotten Son into the world so that we might live through Him. In this is love, not that we loved God, but that He loved us and sent His Son to be the propitiation for our sins. Beloved, if God so loved us, we also ought to love one another. No one has seen God at any time; if we love one another, God abides in us, and His love is perfected in us (1 John 4:7-12 NASB).

See, I think God knew I (and perhaps you) would have a hard time seeing and trusting past the sometimes grandiose theological terms often used to describe Him. All those "omni" words like *omnipotent, omniscient, omnipresent*. Those words are big, majestic, and weighty but not particularly warm or inviting.

But *love?* That word has "come tuck yourself in" written all over it!

Love is the essence of God's nature. It's what He is and what He does—and what He did for you before you became a mother. This divine love blasts out the fear that often keeps us traveling up Guiltmore's guilty slopes. Can you imagine what your life would be like if your thoughts and actions were no longer powered by fear and guilt but rather fueled with confidence and an unshakable trust in the perfect, holy love of God?

Can you *only* imagine?

You don't have to. Right here and right now, you can place your confidence in the love of God the Father—a love so majestic and magnificent that it even dwarfs the love you have for your children.

Character Peg #2: God is consistent (even when we're not).

This has been one of the key pegs that helped me find my way to trusting God. Considering that sometimes I could barely make a decision without second-guessing myself and changing my mind within minutes—well, this aspect of God both intrigues me and fills me with a settled sense of rest. God always responds according to His unchanging nature and character—which, once again, is defined primarily by love.

The book of Malachi states this succinctly: "I the LORD do not change" (3:6 NIV). And King David elaborates:

> In the beginning you laid the foundations of the earth,
>   and the heavens are the work of your hands.
> They will perish...but you remain the same,
>   and your years will never end (Psalm 102:25-27 NIV).

Now this, my friend, is a God I can trust with all my heart, all my mind, all my worries, all my fears, and all my guilt! Why? Because I can trust (and rest) in the unchanging nature and character of God. Absolute consistency is not a realistic goal for me, but God is eternally consistent. I can trust Him to love me dependably and to always keep His word.

Character Peg #3: God is patient (even when we lose patience).

God is God, and I am *so* not.

Think about this for a moment. God has absolute control of Himself and of every minute detail of His creation, including you and me and our children. He is also infinitely patient, which means He never grows tired of us. Never! He is able to listen to our problems, our concerns, our worries, and our regrets over and over and over again. Romans 15:5 refers to Him as "the God of patience and consolation," and His "dependably steady and warmly personal" (MSG) divine character helps develop us to maturity as believers and mothers.

I take great comfort in knowing that God is not impatient like me. He demonstrates patience to those He loves and cares deeply and passionately about. God's patience is tenacious and determined. Nothing can deter Him from His plans. And since He's the God of time, He's not hindered and frustrated by crammed schedules as you and I sometimes are.

God's patient character is also forgiving—a crucial characteristic when dealing with our guilt. Let this Bible truth encourage you: "The Lord is not slow about His promise, as some count slowness, but is patient toward you, not wishing for any to perish but for all to come to repentance" (2 Peter 3:9 NASB).

God is patient toward you—I think those are five of the sweetest and most encouraging words of New Testament truth. So on those days (today being one) when I feel as though I've taken two steps forward and 97 back on the road to Graceland, when I feel like quitting and seriously consider giving up the journey, I can rest in God's patient character, which never once has failed me.

Character Peg #4: God is fair (even when we're not).

When my children were younger, I would often hear one of them whine, "But why does _____ get to _____ and I don't?"

You want to know how I used to answer?

Are you sure?

Well, okay. I used to say with a complete straight face, "Because I love _____ more than you." (Yep, that'll shut 'em up for a second or two!)

I was being facetious, of course. But I have to confess that I have sometimes acted in a decidedly unfair manner as a mother.

How about you?

Have you ever jumped to conclusions and punished a child without getting all the facts? Have you ever found yourself favoring one child over the other or treating one differently—unfairly even—

due to some particular circumstance or simply because that particular child was stepping on every possible nerve he or she possibly could?

If not, you're a saint (and I'm not sure I believe you).

If so, you are far more like me than you may care to be.

But here's the good news. Because of our rather dismal track record of maintaining consistent fairness, we can learn to appreciate all the more the absolute fairness of God. Life itself is not always fair, but the One in charge of life is absolutely just. He cares about what is right, and He doesn't play favorites. He cares for all of us with equal and passionate love. As Isaiah 11:5 (NLT) puts it, God is "clothed with fairness and truth." He can and will sort out what is right when we simply can't.

Character Peg #5: But God is also merciful (thank goodness!).

Fairness is all well and good. It's important. But without the quality of mercy, fairness could be terrifying instead of comforting—especially when we're struggling with guilt.

Think about it. As an imperfect human being and an imperfect mom, do you really want God to give you exactly what you deserve? If He did, none of us would have a chance.

So the Bible goes to great lengths to remind us that the God of fairness and justice is also "gracious, and full of compassion; slow to anger, and of great mercy" (Psalm 145:8). He understands our weaknesses—He created us, remember?—and makes allowances for our imperfection. He gives us chance after chance to get it right, and He forgives our guilty mistakes again and again. We can trust in His mercy even as we keep trying to deserve His justice.

What I've Done Right

Saying "I love you" a million times a day to my baby boy.

—Tammie, age 25

Character Peg #6: God is truth (even when we lose sight of it).
Over the years, Philippians 4:8 has helped us decide which television programs or movies to watch. My children have been guilty of rolling their eyes as soon as I say, "Okay, guys, let's see how it stands against what is true: 'Finally, brothers' [that's you, kids!], 'whatever is true, whatever is noble, whatever is right, whatever is pure, whatever is lovely, whatever is admirable—if anything is excellent or praiseworthy—think about these things' " (NIV).

"Whatever is true"—if we are to rethink the shoulda-woulda-couldas of our guilty past and present, it is imperative that we accept and embrace this hallmark of God's character.

If you have ever heard me speak or read a previous book of mine, you may already know that I have struggled with being a truth teller over the years. I've fudged and hedged on several matters (including issues of mothering) in a vain attempt to deflect responsibility and diminish my own disappointments and hurts, as well as to finagle my way out of situations and circumstances that would leave me smelling like anything but a rose. I've also believed a few lies about myself. And the power of those lies was broken only as a result of speaking, acknowledging, and believing the truth of God's character and His love and desire for me.

What's the biggest lie I've believed about myself? The lie that I know what I'm doing, that I'm capable of being in charge, that I can handle whatever comes.

Which brings me to the second reason that we find it difficult to trust God...

We Trust Ourselves Too Much

I'm not sure any generation of mothers has been inundated with as much information and advice as mine has. Women my age (forty something) cut their maternal teeth on reading material, television talk shows, and parenting gurus (both Christian and non-Christian) who spoon-fed them tons of how-to advice about raising happy, smart, well-adjusted children. What subject pertaining to motherhood hasn't been referenced, footnoted, and copyrighted with the Library of Congress?

And while I am thankful we can turn to the pages of a Penelope Leach book and find out what to do with a clogged milk duct or gather a wealth of pediatric information at the Brazelton Institute website, I think that the sheer amount of information available sometimes makes us moms a little overconfident. We tend to put too much trust in our ability to know the right thing, do the right thing, choose the best thing, or at the very least *research* the best options for every situation.

This rings especially true if you are a research and information addict like me.

"Julie," my husband once told me, "you know more about nothing than anybody I know." I took that as a compliment! Sure, I'd like to think my knowledge is about more than "nothing." But I do want to know as much about everything as I can. And it isn't (just) so I can trump people during conversations or show off while watching *Jeopardy*. I truly love reading. I value information and understanding. I find comfort in knowing who's who and what to do.

And yes, I tend to believe that I can handle anything if I only do my homework.

Truth is, this hunger for information always served me well. It wasn't until well into my mothering career—with the arrival of Patrick Michael Barnhill—that I finally understood the pitfalls of trusting my own knowledge and understanding.

But my first experience with bringing Patrick into the world actually reinforced my cheeky self-confidence. I had read and researched everything I possibly could regarding the birth of my third and final child. And the first matter I looked into was the possibility of having an epidural for this—in case you missed it—my third and *final* labor and delivery. I'd had all the "natural" pain and suffering I could take, thank you very much, and I wasn't a first-time nice mom anymore. I was determined to go through this labor and delivery without fear and loathing.

There was just one small problem with my desire for drugs.

My doctor—nice, kind, soft-spoken Dr. Peachey—informed me that our small local hospital only had one anesthesiologist on call at a time, and so it would not allow elective epidurals.

Well, we'll see about that, I thought.

For the remainder of my time with Dr. Peachey, every time we met, I would ask, "So, Dr. Peachey, have you lined up my epidural yet for the delivery?"

Dr. Peachey would give me a pitying look and then reply, "Well, Julie, I don't know how you're going to manage an epidural. I'd suggest you start praying because it'll take a miracle."

Aha! Something for me to *do*—and something for me to research in a spiritual, praying kind of way! (Maybe I could even write a book titled *The Power of a Praying Pregnant Woman.* Nah…who'd ever buy a book with a title like that?)

I immediately began praying and looking for Bible verses to bring to God's attention—verses that supported my maternal need for pain-numbing drugs, of course. (*Strong's Exhaustive Concordance* doesn't exactly cover this little foray into Scripture.) I also jumped online and looked up elective epidurals, patient's rights, and small hospitals. I even called the hospital and asked if epidurals were allowed for elective *vasectomies.* (Hey, I figured it was worth a shot!)

Meantime, every visit, I would say to Dr. Peachey, "I hope you've got that anesthesiologist lined up, because I'm getting an epidural." I just wouldn't give up. And when I finally arrived at Cottage Hospital in labor and gave my name to the attending nurse, she raised an eyebrow, glanced over to another colleague, and quipped, "Oh, *you're* Julie Barnhill…the one getting the epidural."

Lo and behold, that blessed, dear, wonderful doctor of mine had spoken to Numbing Needle Man, and Numbing Needle Man had assured him if, and only if, no surgeries were scheduled when I arrived for delivery, he would indeed break with hospital convention and induce numbness from my waist to my toes.

And indeed, just before six that morning, I received a glorious injection of something or another (this I didn't research) and spent the next four hours dilating from four to ten centimeters while watching Diane Sawyer host the morning news show—smugly amazed at what a little learning and praying can do!

Weighing in at a robust nine pounds, ten ounces, Patrick was the very picture of health. From the moment of his arrival, his cherubic face and beautifully rounded head begged to be kissed, photographed, and exclaimed over. He was an easy baby, too, sleeping through the night much sooner than either of his siblings had done. I noted that fact in Patrick's baby journal when he was just six weeks old.

Six days later, I was writing an entirely different entry.

Do you remember my confessing that I had once accused Kristen of hurting her baby brother? Well, this is how it happened. Patrick burst out crying as his big sister was holding him. By the time I got to him—a mere four seconds, if that—his face was beet red, and the pupils of his eyes had a terrifyingly gray, fuzzy, unfocused look to them. He looked like he had been choking to death. And while I knew Kristen had not done such a thing, the accusatory tone of my voice caused her to burst out in tears as she stuttered, "Mommy, I didn't do anything to Patrick. He was just sleeping, and then he jerked real hard and started crying."

Boy, did I feel guilty.

So I picked up Patrick and then set Kristen and him both in my lap and told her how much I loved her and what a good sister she was. And all was forgiven and forgotten…until the next day in Aldi's Food Store.

While grocery shopping, I placed Patrick in his baby carrier in the center of my shopping cart. He was sound asleep, and I hoped to get all my purchasing done before he woke. I was just reaching for a bag of sour cream and onion chips when I heard a horrific, guttural choking noise. I looked down and saw my baby's face turn first red and then a bluish hue as he fought for breath.

Instinctively, I picked him up, spoke his name, and gently shook him awake. After what seemed like hours but was really only a second or two, his eyes opened and he let out the loudest and shrillest cry I had ever heard. I cried too, right there in aisle one, when I saw that same eerie, nonfocused, drowning appearance of his eyes. I knew something was wrong—terribly wrong—with my baby, and I wasn't going to rest until I found out what it was.

Immediately I called Dr. Peachey's office and described the events. He said he wasn't too concerned because there hadn't been any "prior events." But he always wanted to err on the side of caution, so he wanted to set Patrick up for an at-home sleep apnea test.

I hung up the phone and thought about the doctor's comment regarding "no prior events." That wasn't true! Suddenly I remembered holding Patrick just a few hours after his birth and attempting to nurse him. As I held him against my breast, he had made a choking noise and seemed to be in distress. I'd pushed the button for the call nurse, but he'd resumed his normal breathing by the time she arrived. The nurse's answer—that he had probably choked on my milk—hadn't set well with me because my milk hadn't even come in yet. But Patrick had appeared to be okay, and the need for sleep soon had overcome my concerns.

Now, seven weeks down the road, all I could do was ask myself over and over again, "Why didn't you ask more questions or do more research about what you saw? How could you have let something so important (and obvious) slip by?"

Apria Home Health did arrive, and Patrick was indeed diagnosed with sleep apnea. In a ten-hour period, he stopped breathing more than 123 times for periods up to 40 seconds. His heart rate slowed significantly during these apnea events—that's what caused the discoloration of skin tone and the muddy, unfocused look in his eyes.

I wrote one thing in his journal that day: "You have apnea. If Kristen hadn't been holding you the day before yesterday or if I had left you with a babysitter while I went grocery shopping, you may have been a SIDS (Sudden Infant Death Syndrome) baby. Thank God for His protection over you, even when I miss the obvious."

Looking at that journal today, I am struck by how utterly convinced I was, even 11 years ago, of my ability to take care of everything as a mom. I didn't lack for confidence. In fact, I suffered from *over*confidence. Only after Patrick's brush with disaster did I realize the limits of my own knowledge and abilities as a mom. (And this was years after my struggles with out-of-control anger!)

That's when I finally began to place my confidence where it truly belonged in the first place—with the God who holds all our lives in His very capable hands.

Regardless of where we find ourselves as mothers, we will always do well to put more trust in God's unfailing character and less confidence, by far, in our own knowledge and abilities. For however intelligent and gifted and talented and informed we may be, we'll eventually come face-to-face with our limitations. We can try and we can learn, but we can do only so much to protect our children.

So does that mean we shouldn't even try? Should we stop worrying about being careful and responsible? Should we stop doing research and learning all we can?

Of course not. There is a balance to be found between trust and responsibility, but unclasping our hold is one of the first steps in finding that balance.

What I've Done Right

Giving my children a good work ethic. I didn't allow them to be lazy or do things halfway. I'm proud to say both of them can be counted on to do a job with excellence.

—Joan, age 37

Learning to Let Go

I recently found myself listening to author Ken Gire speak to a roomful of writers. Mr. Gire doesn't so much speak as lead listeners to a contemplative place of worship and thanksgiving for both the One who has gifted them in one way or another and the unique, individual manner in which this gift works itself out in each one's life. I have to tell you, I believe his ability to do this is part of his own undeniable gift from God.

See, I was sitting in a room full of writers with a capital *W*. I easily could have looked around and been overwhelmed by the sheer number of books many of them have in print.

To my right was a woman who has over a million (yes, one million!) copies of her books in print and writes a minimum of six books *a year*. (I on the other hand have a million book ideas and have actually written six books in my lifetime.) To my left sat another woman who had just received highest honors in the realm of fiction writing. And there were at least 20 others whose famous names would prompt you to ask me, "And you are…?"

In that intimidating situation, it was no small feat for a speaker to get my thoughts off myself and onto something far grander and sublime. But Mr. Gire managed to do just that.

"It is our job to help people pay attention to life…to help them realize something sacred is at stake in every event." Mr. Gire made that observation after we had viewed a poignant clip from the movie *As Good As It Gets*. (Yes, redemptive elements can be found in a Jack Nicholson film.) We looked at a couple more clips and engaged in an enriching discussion about observation and listening. Then, with the intent of sharpening those very powers, Mr. Gire presented a photographic montage of one of history's most famous sculptures: Michelangelo's *Pietà*. This fifteenth-century masterpiece depicts the body of Jesus Christ being cradled and protected in the arms of His earthly mother, Mary.

I had been privileged to view the actual sculpture while touring in Italy many years before, when I was 15 years old. Back then, the *Pietà* was simply one more stop-and-see in a long day of museums and historical buildings. And while I do recall being moved by its beauty, it certainly did not cause me to stop, to observe, and to listen to the echoing chambers of my own heart and mind. That couldn't happen until I had held, loved, cherished, nurtured, and agonized over the life and safety of my own children.

Now, viewing frame after frame of photographs taken at every angle imaginable, I was mesmerized by the stunning detail of Michelangelo's work.

Christ's body—limp in His mother's lap, projecting both the pathos of death and the powerful possibility of resurrection.

Mary's form—her flowing garments suggesting a burial shroud for her son, the very tilt of her body suggesting the emptiness of bereavement, the power of nurturing love, and a flicker of faithful hope.

And Mary's hands—something I had never paid attention to before. As I looked at them now, I understood something about what it means to balance trust with responsibility for my children.

The right hand of Michelangelo's Mary is tucked beneath her son's right shoulder. The fingers are taut, holding her baby's slumped body in a fiercely protective grip. But Mary's left hand is gently extended to the side, palm up, as if in motherly surrender. As if to relinquish the One she loves so dearly.

It was the contrast of those hands as presented through the work of Michelangelo that spoke to me that day.

One clenched tight with protective love.

The other opened as an offering of trust.

This is where I believe we all find ourselves. And this is the attitude I ask you to consider as you listen to and observe your own sacred journey.

What is the position of your own hands—the disposition of your heart, my sweet friend, as you hold on to your children? What do you do with your dreams and longings as a mother, the broken promises, the inevitable disappointments, and yes, the guilt that the mothering role inevitably entails?

Can you identify with my observations of Mary, the mother of Jesus? Can you manage to hold on tight to the ones you love while also relaxing your grip and trusting them to One who loves them even better and more capably than you do?

If you're like me, that's something you still might need to work on. But it's worth the try. And you really are almost there.

12
Traveling Light

Hiking with Heart and Humor and Humility

◎

It's been a long trip, hasn't it?

All the way up into Guiltmore National Park—across the foot-hills of Wasgonnabe, up the slopes of Shoulda, Coulda, Woulda, Inconsistency, and even Unimaginable...with Immaculate Perfection always in sight and out of reach. Then downhill through the rocky back slopes—passing up tempting shortcuts in favor of the difficult but rewarding trail of confession, forgiveness, and making amends. Learning along the way some hard but fulfilling lessons of trust and relinquishment.

But even as we cross the border into Graceland (which looks sus-piciously like home in a better light), I want to remind you that you'll be making other treks through Guiltmore from time to time. That's just the way things are.

Because of our trip together, though, I hope we'll both be making these repeat treks with a lot less old, unresolved guilt. I hope you realize, as I do, how much better it all goes with a little company, a little wisdom and experience, and a lot of divine help. And I hope you've discovered the importance of always staying warm and trav-eling light.

With that in mind, as we wind up our journey together, I'd like to recommend some basic equipment and supplies that can make it all a little easier.

If we were climbing an actual mountain range, I'd recommend you bring along sturdy boots, warm but breathable socks, rain protection, dehydrated food, and an all-purpose knife. But for this metaphorical hike, I suggest we pay attention to a phrase I heard long ago in a Joni Mitchell song. What we need to travel more comfortably through Guiltmore are extra doses of "heart and humor and humility."

Here's what I mean.

Hiking with Heart: Loving Connections That Lighten Your Step

One of the first things you learn about being a mom is that little things really do mean a lot. And little acts of connection between two hearts can make even the trek over Guiltmore's rocky crags seem not only worthwhile but easier.

You know what I mean. They're the same little moments that can make a mother's heart sing.

A single sticky hug from a toddler.

A whispered "I love you, Mommy" at bedtime.

An affirming touch from your husband when you are really at your wit's end (or better yet, an offer to hold down the fort while you grab a few minutes for yourself).

A quick, encouraging cup of coffee with another mom who has been where you are now and lived to tell about it.

Or how about one of those rare moments in the car when your teen actually pulls off the headphones and tells you what's on his mind? (Be still, my heart.)

They're what keep us going—those treasured moments of sharing and affection, those times when heart connects to heart. And the more of these you initiate, the more of them you open your heart to, the more of them you gather in your memory…the easier your future treks through Guiltmore will be.

The reason for this is that heart connections tend to generate emotional and spiritual energy, while guilt feelings tend to be energy drains. So filling your life with affirmation, affection, and support helps counteract the work of coping with guilt. To me, it's a little like loading your pack with trail mix and lightweight power bars— perfect sustenance for those inevitable treks through Guiltmore.

So how can we stock up on the connections in our lives? Here are a few ideas that even the busiest mom can try.

Heart Connector #1: Give a compliment.

This is one of the easiest and quickest way to add a spark of heart to your day. Simply look around for someone who is doing or wearing or saying something you like—and tell him or her what you think. Catch your ten-year-old in an act of kindness and don't be stingy with the praise. Tell a store clerk you like her sweater. Thank your Bible study leader for a well-prepared lesson. You don't have to butter people up or be insincere. Just try to get in the habit of noticing good things around you and commenting on them. You'll give others a boost—and yourself as well.

Heart Connector #2: Reach out and touch.

We saw back in chapter 6 that physical touch is a primal language of love. Children in particular need touch to thrive. Research shows that children who are freely hugged, kissed, and cuddled by their parents are healthier, better adjusted, and generally happier than the ones whose parents are less physically demonstrative. And even the smallest children understand the language of touch—the language of love. So one of the most effective ways to build your heart connections is through the gift of touch. You can do this even if you're not the touchy-feely type. Start today—in the smallest or biggest way you can—and begin finding more ways to demonstrate the inward love and devotion you feel toward each of your children.

You might want to start with a simple kiss to the forehead. Or reach your hand over across the seat while you are driving and hold on to the child riding in the front seat with you. I did this with all three of my kids. And even now, one of the older ones might occasionally slip a hand over and give my arm a quick squeeze. (Don't tell anyone I told you this. My kids would be mortified!)

Our children often talk much more readily if we encourage them with our touch. Before diving into a conversation, think of how you might be able to reassure your son or daughter of your interest by a quick pat on the arm or a firm but gentle hug. Touch can be a strong *silent* communication that is sometimes more effective than words. Your three-year-old who has fallen and hurt herself will be comforted by your hug, as will her sixteen-year-old sister who has been hurt emotionally.

You don't need to reserve touch for your children of course. Most of your heart connections can be enhanced by touch—a hand on a friend's shoulder, a quick hug at church, a neck rub or hand massage for someone who is feeling stressed. And don't forget to include your husband in your efforts to reach out and touch. Your marriage needs both intimate touch and casual, loving touch to remain healthy.

Obviously, whenever you reach out to touch someone, you should be sensitive to the other person and not force the contact. Some people, for reasons ranging from arthritis to autism to emotional trauma, find physical touch to be painful or overwhelming. And your children may go through stages when they resist Mom's enthusiastic hugs.

Even when people resist touch, however, they usually still need it in some form. The key is to be both respectful and creative. If someone shrinks away from physical contact, try something a little less intrusive, like a gentle touch of the hand. Or try something a friend of mine tried during her daughter's "touch me not" phase. She insisted, with humor, on a "handshake goodnight." That minimal contact during a tricky period was enough to sustain and build the heartfelt connection between her and her daughter.

Heart Connector # 3: Surprise your family with random acts of extravagant love.

If you're like most moms, you spend most of your days giving to those you love—cooking meals, running errands, kissing boo-boos, doling out hugs and words of encouragement. But you can give an extra boost to your family—yourself included—with an occasional act of extra, extravagant love.

Maybe you could pick up your son from school and take him to an amusement park—just the two of you. Or treat your daughter's favorite poster to a new frame. Or pull out your piggybank to buy the car stereo your husband has been wanting for months but couldn't justify. Or let everyone eat ice cream for dinner (not just dessert). Or borrow a great idea from Donna Otto's book *Finding Your Purpose As a Mom* and occasionally proclaim a "grace day" when kids are excused from their regular chores.[7] The details of what you do don't really matter. What matters are the heart connections and the memories you build with such special acts of love.

Heart Connector #4: Don't neglect your network.

I never could have made it through the children-at-home mothering years without my friends—church friends, work colleagues, fellow moms, and old friends who have kept up with me over the years. The support and love of those who hiked alongside me and those who supported me with prayers and casseroles and heartfelt conversation has made all the difference as I came home from Guiltmore. I like to think I've done the same for them.

And yet in the hectic rush of family life, we can easily get in the habit of putting friendships on hold. Sometimes that's simply necessary—and good friends understand. At the same time, a little friendship maintenance can do a lot to lighten your load—both because you keep your support network healthy and because you don't add extra guilt for neglecting your friends!

It really doesn't take much. An occasional phone call can keep a friendship going until you have more time. An offer to team up on home chores—"We'll hang your curtains and then you can help me paint"—can let you catch up while getting your work done. A loving note, a funny "I miss you" card, or even a quick e-mail can say "I'm still thinking of you." And of course from time to time you'll need to stop everything to be there for a friend in need.

Whatever you do, whatever is needed—the effort is worth it. You *need* your friends, not only to get off Guiltmore but to make it through your life. They need you too. That's the way it's supposed to be!

Heart Connector #5: Involve your family in loving outreach.

God made us in such way that reaching out to others actually lightens our own hearts—not to mention reducing our load of guilt. This is a truth that you need to remember and your kids need to learn. So why not add to your "heart" supply by working together as a family to make a difference in the world? This effort can be as simple as buying dog food at the grocery store to donate to the Humane Society or purchasing a meal for the homeless guy on the corner. It can be as complicated as volunteering together on an overseas mission trip. Or it can be anything in between—visiting a nursing home, serving soup at a homeless shelter, or knitting blankets for a children's home.

Obviously, you can't meet every need, but you can build heart connections by becoming part of the solution.

What I've Done Right

I always kept a huge box of Band-Aids on a low shelf for my children to use. I rarely told them, "You don't need a Band-Aid!" Instead, I would let them put two, three, even four, on their gnat-sized scratch and then kiss it and tell them I loved them. It was worth every penny I spent at the drugstore.

—Pam, age 47

Heart Connector #6: Keep your mind and your heart open for gifts of grace.

The truth is, most moments of heartfelt connection will not be those you create. They are gifts of pure grace that light on you without notice. Sometimes they'll come when you're at your worst, all but overwhelmed with stress or worry or guilt. Just when you're ready to give up, when your whole being is screaming for help, you'll be granted a time out, a distraction, a moment of calm, a flash of insight, or perhaps one of those sticky hugs.

You can't control moments like that. You can't make them happen. But you can respond. You can welcome them with open arms and a deep, grateful breath. You can whisper "Thank you" and "I love you." And you can remember that this gift of a moment comes courtesy of One who loves you and wants to supply your need.

Never forget, God *wants* you to live in Graceland, not on Guiltmore. He'll give you the heart you need to get down off the mountain one more time.

Hiking with Humor: Lightening Your Load with Laughter

Tell me what a woman laughs at or about, and I'll tell you a thing or two about that woman.

Take me for instance.

Tacked to a two-by-three-foot corkboard hanging just above the work space my family often refers to as the Bat Cave are random quotes, cards, photographs, and miscellaneous items that are sure to bring a laugh, if not a guffaw, from my lips.

The first item is a folksy painted plaque dangling precipitously from the center of the board. On it is written the following quote: "I love deadlines! I especially love the swooshing sound they make as they go flying by."

Now that makes me laugh. And it probably makes my publisher and editor very nervous.

Just above the plaque is an oversized card that declares, "If you're not going to *snort*, why even laugh?" It's signed by two of my friends who share my oversized sense of humor.

To the right of the card is a photograph of Patrick during his first Christmas. He stands facing the camera, clutching a stuffed reindeer while wearing a pair of snuggly red sweat pants bunched about his knees and a wrinkled casual shirt about two sizes too big that he had dug out of Ricky's closet (um, more like off his floor) and demanded he button up "all by myself" (that Mercer Mayer book was nearly the death of me!). Wrapping paper is strewn all about his feet, and a box lies half open as he impishly grins for posterity's sake.

I love that photo, and I can't look at it without chuckling out loud.

To the right of Patrick's photo is an outrageous caricature of me created by an artist at one of Harvest House Publishers' fabulous Christian Booksellers Association parties. I had observed the drawings he created earlier, and when I sat down I told him, "Make mine big and brassy, nothing ho-hum. Something that really gets your attention."

Well, he did what I asked. I…er, *they* are indeed big and brassy. My girlfriends and fellow Harvest House authors Pam Farrel, Jill Savage, and Lysa TerKeurst all busted a gut upon viewing the far-from-ho-hum proportions of my image. That's why I have it proudly tacked to the cork board and not displayed in my living room! Besides, every time it catches my eye, I laugh. Out loud.

Because each time my eye catches a glimpse of that black-and-white drawing, I think about the expressions on Pam, Jill, and Lysa's faces when I showed it to them. I was somewhat oblivious to the obvious, but they weren't. And their hysterical comments had me laughing so hard I had to bend over and hold my aching stomach muscles. So that picture reminds me just how good it felt to be a jumping off place for others to laugh so hard they snorted.

My point is, laughter is a powerful tool that we as mothers would do well to utilize.

It has the power to diffuse tense and potentially explosive situations.

It is essential to ensure long-lasting, healthy relationships with family, friends, and coworkers.

Laughter is important to your health too. It releases chemicals called endorphins, which give us a feeling of relief. In fact, researchers estimate that laughing a hundred times a day is equal to a ten-minute workout on a rowing machine. Laughter decreases blood pressure and increases the blood flow to your heart and the level of oxygen in your blood. It gives your diaphragm, abs, and back muscles a true workout, not to mention your respiratory system and facial muscles. (No wonder my sides hurt so bad after a raucous round of guffawing and snorting!) Can you imagine the incredible shape our body, mind, and soul would be in if we only disciplined ourselves and "worked out" every day with laughter?

What would happen if we purposely set out each and every day to take ourselves and even our guilty shoulda-woulda-couldas a little less seriously? What would happen if we paid as much careful attention to our daily outgo of laughter as we did our daily intake of carbohydrates, calories, or fat grams? You know what I think would transpire? I think we'd live with a lot less guilt. We'd deal with what guilt we have in a much healthier way. And our families would be a lot happier with a more laugh-prone mom.

Consider this, Mom. Did you know the average adult only laughs 14 times a day? Just 14 times? Goodness! I get the shivers just typing that in. But the number doesn't really surprise me because life often seems to get less funny as we get weighed down with such grown-up responsibilities as jobs, kids, mortgages (or rent), and gasoline prices.

Especially gas prices, which happen to have shot up by nearly a dollar in the months when I was writing this book.

In fact, the other day I declared a moratorium on conversations about the skyrocketing cost of gasoline. It seemed like the first thing and the last thing we talked about when driving to Kristen's volleyball games, Ricky Neal's football scrimmages, or Patrick's football league tournaments was the current, depressing cost of a gallon of gas. I couldn't remember laughing—truly laughing—with my husband for more than two weeks.

Now, I'm not opposed to relevant cultural conversations, mind you, and I'm always happy to put in my two cents' worth regarding oil companies, the Middle East, and price gouging. But two weeks of mutual complaints about gas prices—let me tell you, that made for some less-than-jovial bantering.

The endorphins were dropping like flies, so I mandated more fun and less gasoline angst. A few nights later we watched an old Mel Brooks movie that neither of us remembered seeing, and we both laughed so hard we cried.

Now, my husband, Rick, isn't much of a verbal laugher. He's got one of those wonderful, silent, scrunch-your-face laughs that always tends to set me off as well. In fact, just watching him laugh can get me laughing so hard that I need a Depends undergarment for backup.

That, my friend, is the way I believe God intended for husbands and wives to spend their time—laughing with one another as opposed to lamenting and wearing sackcloth while pilfering through loose change for gasoline funds.

And here's the marvelous thing about adding humor and laughter to your life as an adult and a woman—it naturally trickles down into your life as a mom. I know when I am maintaining a healthy diet of reading humorous writing, viewing hilarious movies, and hanging out with adult-diaper-inspiring girlfriends—well, my kids reap the benefits. I'm more prone to laugh with them and to pick up the subtle nuances of preadolescent humor.

And here's another bonus: When I make laughter a priority in my adult life, it becomes a priority in my life with the children. And trust me—when you're living with kids, the more humor the better! So here are a few suggestions for lightening up as a family:

Laugh Lightener #1: Encourage your kids to bring home jokes... and laugh at them (the jokes, not the kids!).

For those moms reading these pages whose children are older than seven, you know how important this is. And how excruciatingly painful it can be to do. Especially when the joke goes something like this:

> *Child:* Knock, knock.
> *Mom:* Who's there?
> *Child:* What.
> *Mom:* What who?
> *Child:* Dog.

But you laugh. Yes, laugh. And she repeats it five, ten, twenty times and then says, "Hey, Mom! I got a *new* joke."

Child: Knock, knock.
Mom: Who's there?
Child: Why.
Mom: Why who?
Child: Dog.

But you carry on. Eyes glued to the road before you, hands gripped to the steering wheel, as an Anita Renfroe comedic genius wannabe is born.

Hang on, Mom, it's worth it. Laughing with your children encourages imagination and creativity and keeps the home atmosphere light. And chances are, with time, the jokes really will get better.

Laugh Lightener #2: Laugh at your own jokes (even if others don't).

About five or six years ago I was sitting at the dinner table with my husband and children when I said something I found to be terribly funny, and before I could barely finish my comment, I was laughing so hard I spit food. I apologized (sort of—I was laughing too hard to enunciate properly) and I noticed no one was laughing but me.

About that time Rick (the straight man foil for much of my humor) looked at the children, paused for dramatic effect, and then said,

"You kids realize your mom was an only child, right?"

Bar-ah-ah!

And I spit some more.

I can appreciate the fact that not everyone finds me amusing. But I've never been shy to laugh when I think something I said or observed is funny. And I don't want any of you to shy away from it either. I want you to seize the power and thrill of being your greatest fan...and reap the guilt-free benefits of whatever makes you laugh.

What I've Done Right

Teaching my daughters how to sew, bake homemade bread, and arrange flowers.

—Debbie, age 39

Laugh Lightener #3: Teach through example that's it's good to laugh at yourself.

This isn't quite the same thing as laughing at your own jokes. This piece of advice has to do with being able to appreciate the absurdity of your own life—and to milk that absurdity for all its comedic worth! It's also a prerequisite to humility, so it packs a double whammy in terms of traveling light. Try it!

Laugh Lightener #4: Create a humor library.

Start clipping cartoons and posting them on a bulletin board or the refrigerator. Purchase calendars and greeting cards that tickle your funny bone, or listen to great comedy on CD or DVD as a family. And don't forget to buy your kids a new joke book! Collect whatever you can to promote a healthy lifestyle of laughter for you individually and for your family as well.

Laugh Lightener #5: Let your children see you laugh.

The truth is, laughter is contagious. The habit of healthy laughter can also be taught. So if your kids tickle your funny bone, don't always hold in the chortles. And make sure they see you laugh with others too so they know that humor is part of everyday interaction. Seeing you laugh with others compels your own children to do the same. So put this book down and call up a funny friend or two and invite them over for dinner or dessert. Laugh, laugh, laugh—and encourage your children to invite a few of their funny friends as well.

Hiking with Humility: The Joy of Keeping Things Real

Here's a basic rule of thumb that can really help you keep things light on the guilt trail. You'll reduce your guilt load by a lot if you remember who you are.

By this I mean you're not God. You're not perfect. You're not *expected* to be perfect.

As I said…basic. But this basic realization helps you hold on to one of your most useful climbing tools.

I'm talking about humility. A humble attitude. A realistic self-assessment. A willingness to admit your own foibles (even laugh at them) and then accept help.

Such an attitude keeps us all a bit more real, less guilt-ridden, and a little less obnoxious.

Obnoxious? Let me explain.

I will be the first to admit that had I *not* become a mother I would have, in all likelihood, turned out to be an irritating and irksome writer/speaker/woman who thinks she knows it all and who writes books and delivers speeches to prove it. (Okay…I would have been *more* irritating and irksome.) This tendency may have something to do with my natural inclination to be an all-or-nothing thinker. Before I had children, that all-or-nothing thinking tended to be pretty matter-of-fact, cut-and-dried, and more than a little judgmental.

And this included parenting issues, which I knew nothing about, of course.

I remember doling out advice and espousing all sorts of profound statements (often quietly in the confines of my own mind) as I watched mothers handle their babies, toddlers, children, and teens.

Is the baby fussing and crying and keeping you and your husband awake? Let him cry it out, and just learn to sleep over the sound.

Is your three-year-old butting his head against your thigh in the middle of K-Mart? Tell him to stop.

Still having trouble fitting into your pre-pregnancy jeans—when the baby turned 13 years old yesterday? Show a little discipline, for Pete's sake!

I'd go on, but it's too embarrassing.

Obnoxious, huh?

But luckily for me and you, I did have children! And with each baby I brought home, my level of knowing it all decreased, and my understanding of the need for a humble attitude and mind-set increased.

How could it not? It's not as if we can opt out of humility once we take on the task of mothering. Oh, no, it comes prepackaged and ready to serve, just like those samples of Enfamil formula you brought home from the hospital. The use of which, you may have believed, would guarantee that your child would develop the IQ of a gnat.

I know. I had a complete emotional breakdown on day 15, after Kristen's birth. I hurt, "the girls" hurt, Kristen was losing weight, and I just knew a lack of breast milk was going to take her out of contention for any future gifted and talented programs.

But guess what? I learned better. And I learned that motherhood ushers in (often with trumpets!) a dawning awareness that things just aren't going to go as we had first planned or imagined. As such, it allows us the opportunity not to always have to be right, or better, or more prepared, or more in control.

Being a mother allows us ample opportunities to embrace humility.

It helps us establish stronger and stronger heart connections.

If we let it, motherhood will always provide us with reasons to laugh.

What a great thought!

Motherhood may be a dependable source of guilt—and it seems to be mandatory for every mom to spend some time hiking on Guiltmore.

At the same time, God uses the experience of motherhood to provide us with a steady supply of what we need to leave Guiltmore in the distance and keep on moving lightly down the road.

13

Peace in the Valley

Putting Guiltmore in the Distance

◎

*W*ell, we're here…and can you believe how beautiful it is?

Just take a look at the trail beneath our feet for starters.

It's good, solid, well-compressed soil, with nary a rock or rut to be seen. Its grade is gentle and rolling instead of steep and treacherous. And it's more than wide enough for you and me to walk side by side again, enjoying the green and pleasant landscape. You don't need Sherpa Mom to scout ahead. Through diligence and divine grace, we have made our way down and are able once again to amble comfortably along. The rocky slopes of Guiltmore National Park are far behind us now.

Go ahead, take a deep breath and take another appreciative look around. See how the air sparkles? See how the sun smiles on the riverbanks? See the wind rustling the willow branches?

It's the place you have dreamed of for so long—the peaceful valley of Graceland.

And you know what the funny thing is? This valley of grace was never as far from us as we may have believed.

I'm smiling as I write this because life has once again provided the perfect wrap-up story. You see, a little less than a week ago, Kristen was fighting a sore throat, running a low-grade fever, and growing more and more frustrated by a dragging fatigue. Now, having read this book and gotten to know me pretty well, you probably know what I did.

Yep, I went online, Googled her symptoms, and declared that she was in all likelihood fighting mononucleosis. Rick thought I might be jumping to diagnostic conclusions but agreed she needed to see a doctor. Dr. Peachey was out of town, so she was examined by another physician—a perfectly nice man, mind you, but no Dr. Peachey.

He listened to her heart, checked her reflexes, declared she had a virus, and sent her home with instructions to take Tylenol for the fever and to rest.

I was none too happy with his diagnostic conclusions, but I couldn't do much at that point. So we went home, and I began to pack for a weekend speaking event.

I left on Thursday morning, did my speaking, and started back home on Sunday afternoon. And as I sat at the gate of an America West flight in Phoenix, Arizona, I listened to the one voice message left on my cell phone the morning before.

It was Kristen, and she was crying.

Her symptoms had mushroomed once I left. She was running a high fever now, and her throat was so sore she could barely speak, but still she left me this desperate message: "Mom, I feel awful. When will you be home to take care of me?"

What I've Done Right

Creating a love and desire for knowing the Bible.

—Gloria, age 44

Needless to say, my stomach clenched when I heard that.

The problem was that the America West flight had just been delayed for the third time. I wouldn't be arriving back home in Illinois until around six thirty Monday morning.

I listened to Kristen's message four times.

She sounded like she was about four years old. Every mom cell in my body wanted to commandeer the nearest jet and do whatever was necessary to be there for her.

My baby needed me. She longed for my presence. But I couldn't get to her.

Can you say *guilt?*

And yes, the old shoulda-coulda-wouldas immediately began clamoring inside me. I shoulda cancelled my speaking engagement and stayed home with her. I coulda insisted that Rick take her to the doctor again on Friday.

But then the funniest, most ironic thing happened.

As I mulled over familiar, wrenching, guilty feelings, I lifted my eyes, looked out the concourse windows, and saw the Sierra Estrella mountain range sitting smack dab in the airport's backyard!

I couldn't believe it. Guiltmore had followed me clear across the country!

I found myself shaking my head and chuckling aloud as I then pulled out my edited manuscript and reread the closing statements of chapter 1:

> I consider guilt, with all its intrinsic ties to maternal life and love, to be a vast, take-your-breath-away, geographical landscape that will sit squarely in my backyard until the day I die…That's why I make no promises of "conquer your guilt" or "break free forever and ever" within the pages of this book. I am *so* over thinking I

can do the impossible—and then feeling even guiltier when I cannot.

Yes, guilt will always be part of the mothering landscape.

But pay attention, because this is important: It doesn't have to *dominate* your landscape. It doesn't have to ruin your life, or spoil your fun, or rob you of peace of mind. More important, it doesn't have to erode your confidence and cripple your effectiveness as a mother and a human being.

Instead of hunkering down under Guiltmore's shadow, you can learn to scale her slopes and move on to where you were really meant to live—on the sunny plains of grace and confidence.

And from there—take it from me—the view is really terrific.

Well, guess what, moms? Every word I wrote back then is still true! We still can't hide from Guiltmore. But the view from this valley (or this airport) is better than we ever dreamed.

Because even though Guiltmore was sitting as big as could be in my traveling backyard on that Sunday afternoon, I didn't respond to it the way I used to. Instead of meandering its trails or racing toward its guilty peaks, I stopped and thought a thing or two. I reminded myself of several points of truth,

- I was contractually obligated to attend the event.

- I can't do anything about the delayed flights.

- My husband is perfectly capable of nurturing and taking care of our daughter.

- Taking on feelings of false guilt isn't going to get me home to Kristen any sooner or aid in her physical healing.

- God loves my daughter more than I do and will take care of both of us.

And that was it. I was already putting Guiltmore behind me. I was tempted to do a guilt-free happy dance at gate B23, but instead I chose to celebrate by purchasing a congratulatory Whopper with cheese at the Burger King kiosk.

You see, it does my heart good to know the words I have written and the time you have taken to read them counts for something!

It *is* possible to climb down from Guiltmore's peaks and to walk and live in the valley of peace with vistas of grace spreading out around us.

It *is* possible to retrain your mind, your heart, and your memories and to purposefully choose to believe, to feel, and to act in a guilt-free manner.

It *is* possible not only to recognize those looming peaks but to find your way off of their slopes far more quickly and effectively than you have in the past.

It *is* possible to avoid an avalanche of mixed feelings and say no to false guilt.

It *is* possible to own up to true guilt and by God's grace and purposeful intent to walk in freedom away from it.

Most important, it is possible for each and every one of us who have journeyed off Guiltmore's peaks to lead at least one more guilt-addled mom here to the valley of peace.

Together we scaled the peaks of Guiltmore National Park.

Today, together, we can choose to live in grace.

Notes

1. Julie Ann Barnhill, *She's Gonna Blow! Real Help for Moms Dealing with Anger* (Eugene, OR: Harvest House, 2001/2005).

2. You can calculate all sorts of highlights at the time and date website: http://www.timeanddate.com/date/duration.html.

3. Lisa Jackson, "Kiss Guilt Goodbye," *Christian Parenting Today*, September/October 1999, p. 466. Accessed online at www.christianitytoday.com/cpt/9g5/9g5044.html, October 18, 2005.

4. Debra Manchester, "Saving My Sanity: Why Writing Makes Me a Better Mom," *WebMomz*, http://www.webmomz.com/Business-Articles/why-i-write.shtml (accessed June 2005).

5. Julie Ann Barnhill, *'Til Debt Do Us Part* (Eugene, OR: Harvest House, 2002); *Scandalous Grace* (Wheaton, IL: Tyndale House, 2004); *Radical Forgiveness* (Wheaton, IL: Tyndale House, 2005); *Exquisite Hope* (Wheaton, IL: Tyndale House, 2005).

6. Lewis B. Smedes, *Forgive & Forget: Healing the Hurts We Don't Deserve* (San Francisco: HarperSanFrancisco, 1996).

7. Donna Otto with Anne Christian Buchanan, *Finding Your Purpose as a Mom: How to Build Your Home on Holy Ground* (Eugene, OR: Harvest House, 2004), 184-85.

You can visit Julie Ann Barnhill's website at
www.juliebarnhill.com

To write to Julie:

Julie Barnhill
c/o Harvest House Publishers
990 Owen Loop N.
Eugene, OR 97402-9173

*If you are interested in having
Julie speak at your special
event, please contact:*

309-335-7941

Email: julie@juliebarnhill.com

Facebook: Julie Patrick-Barnhill